"To the extent that ⟨...⟩eself in an alien (client) environment ⟨...⟩ relational dynamics of that setting, it represents a derivative – albeit commercial – form of ethnography. What better method, then, to explore the practice of consultancy itself? Furthermore, and as the editors of this volume rightly observe, the complexity and uncertainty of everyday consultancy life belies the orderliness and linearity of consultancy technique prescribed in mainstream management literature. The (auto)ethnographic methods advanced collectively by the contributors of this book takes aim at this tension. This volume makes for a read that is genuinely insightful, rewarding, and pedagogically rich."

Dr. Tom Vine, *Associate Professor, University of Suffolk, and editor,*
Ethnographic Research and Analysis: Anxiety, Identity and Self

"This timely book is for reflective managers as well as consultants who are unconvinced or disillusioned by conventional wisdom. It proposes a 'grown up' approach that moves away from the easy idealizations and simplifications of organizational realities and consultancy interventions. Based upon insights born of curiosity and lived experience, each chapter deals with the 'dirt' and explores the 'shadows' of organizing and managing. Emphasizing the importance of increased self-understanding and deeper sense-making, this path-breaking book urges and advances the adoption of more thoughtful, less self-defeating means of grappling with the demanding, contradictory practices of managing and consulting."

Prof. Hugh Willmott, *Bayes Business School*

"How stimulating to encounter a text that probes those discomforting experiences that arise during consulting processes, and, rather than explaining them away or trying to avoid them, shows how discussing these frankly and thoughtfully unearths a fertile ground for informing ethical action."

Dr. Patricia Shaw, *Co-founder of the Doctor of Management*
Programme at University of Hertfordshire

"A unique book, based in the autoethnographic experience of its contributors, this collection provides a richly nuanced and reflexively theorised insight into the complex reality of everyday consultancy practice. It is essential reading for practitioners, researchers and students."

Prof. Ian Burkitt, *University of Bradford*

THE COMPLEXITY OF CONSULTANCY

Consultancy is a lucrative industry dependent on the production and use of tools and techniques which hold out the promise of success for the organisations it supports: transformation, or greater efficiency and effectiveness, perhaps even culture change. However, a critical and important question is whether these promises are fulfilled in everyday practice in organisations. Is it possible at all for consultants to predict and control the changes that their clients ask for? This volume reframes the role of consultants from detached observers wielding a stable body of knowledge useful in all contexts, to that of skilled participants in the conscious and unconscious processes of organisational life.

In this book, one of three in a series looking at complexity and management, the expert authors bring together their experiences to provide vibrant accounts of how to lead in everyday organisational situations using practical judgement. The book includes a brief historical introduction to complexity and leadership, real-world narratives illustrating concrete dilemmas in the workplace, and a concluding chapter that draws together the practical and theoretical implications.

With both theoretical grounding and practical insights from managers and consultants in leading firms, this is an ideal resource for executives and students on leadership development and talent management programmes, as well as those undertaking higher education courses in leadership and consulting.

Nicholas Sarra works as a Consultant Psychotherapist within the NHS. He is also a Visiting Professor at Hertfordshire Business School, University of Hertfordshire, and affiliated with a number of programmes at Exeter University. He is a member of the Institute of Group Analysis.

Karina Solsø is a Self-employed Organisational Consultant in Denmark working with organisational change and leadership development. She is also a Visiting Lecturer at Hertfordshire Business School, University of Hertfordshire.

Chris Mowles is Professor of Complexity and Management at Hertfordshire Business School, University of Hertfordshire.

Complexity and Management

Series Editor: Chris Mowles, University of Hertfordshire, UK

The Complexity of Consultancy
Exploring Breakdowns within Consultancy Practice
Edited by Nicholas Sarra, Karina Solsø and Chris Mowles

Complexity and Leadership
Edited by Kiran Chauhan, Emma Crewe and Chris Mowles

Complexity and the Public Sector
Edited by Chris Mowles and Karen Norman

For more information about this series, please visit: www.routledge.com/Complexity-and-Management/book-series/CM

THE COMPLEXITY OF CONSULTANCY

Exploring Breakdowns Within Consultancy Practice

Edited by
Nicholas Sarra,
Karina Solsø and Chris Mowles

LONDON AND NEW YORK

Cover image: Getty Images / Giorez

First published 2023
by Routledge
4 Park Square, Milton Park, Abingdon, Oxon OX14 4RN

and by Routledge
605 Third Avenue, New York, NY 10158

Routledge is an imprint of the Taylor & Francis Group, an informa business

© 2023 selection and editorial matter, Nicholas Sarra, Karina Solsø and Chris Mowles; individual chapters, the contributors

The right of Nicholas Sarra, Karina Solsø and Chris Mowles to be identified as the authors of the editorial material, and of the authors for their individual chapters, has been asserted in accordance with sections 77 and 78 of the Copyright, Designs and Patents Act 1988.

All rights reserved. No part of this book may be reprinted or reproduced or utilised in any form or by any electronic, mechanical, or other means, now known or hereafter invented, including photocopying and recording, or in any information storage or retrieval system, without permission in writing from the publishers.

Trademark notice: Product or corporate names may be trademarks or registered trademarks, and are used only for identification and explanation without intent to infringe.

British Library Cataloguing-in-Publication Data
A catalogue record for this book is available from the British Library

Library of Congress Cataloging-in-Publication Data
Names: Sarra, Nicholas, editor. | Solsø, Karina, editor. | Mowles, Chris, editor.
Title: The complexity of consultancy : exploring breakdowns within consultancy practice / edited by Nicholas Sarra, Karina Solsø and Chris Mowles.
Description: Milton Park, Abingdon, Oxon ; New York, NY : Routledge, 2023. | Series: Complexity and management | Includes bibliographical references and index.
Identifiers: LCCN 2022011265 (print) | LCCN 2022011266 (ebook) Subjects: LCSH: Business consultants. | Management. | Leadership.
Classification: LCC HD69.C6 C5866 2023 (print) | LCC HD69.C6 (ebook) | DDC 658.4/6–dc23/eng/20220314
LC record available at https://lccn.loc.gov/2022011265
LC ebook record available at https://lccn.loc.gov/2022011266

ISBN: 978-0-367-54470-6 (hbk)
ISBN: 978-0-367-55980-9 (pbk)
ISBN: 978-1-003-09594-1 (ebk)

DOI: 10.4324/9781003095941

Typeset in Joanna
by codeMantra

CONTENTS

List of contributors ix
Preface to the Complexity and Management series: The key ideas of complex responsive processes of relating and their recent development xi
Acknowledgements xxi

Introduction 1
KARINA SOLSØ AND NICHOLAS SARRA

1 **Moving beyond neutrality: recognising the moral agency of the consultant through reflexive inquiries into shame** 16
KIRAN CHAUHAN

2 **Consulting: facilitation and shame: working together to avoid challenges to our sense of self in the recognition of others** 38
GRAHAM CURTIS

3 **What are consultants actually recognised for?** 60
ERIC WENZEL

4	**Actualising plurality: an Arendtian perspective on responding to powerlessness and loss of freedom** KARINA SOLSØ	83
5	**Collaboration as a politics of affect** ROBBERT MASSELINK	105
6	**Selling ourselves short: marketing the self strategically: towards success beyond recognition** JACQUELINE JANSSEN	127
	Conclusion: summarizing reflections on the practice of consultancy KARINA SOLSØ AND NICHOLAS SARRA	153
	Index	163

CONTRIBUTORS

Kiran Chauhan is an Organisational Consultant at The King's Fund, a health and care policy think tank in the UK. He is also a Visiting Lecturer at Hertfordshire Business School, University of Hertfordshire, UK. Kiran graduated as Doctor of Management from the University of Hertfordshire in 2019.

Graham Curtis is a Senior Organisation Development Consultant at Roffey Park Institute, an organisation, leadership and executive development centre based in Sussex, UK. Graham graduated as Doctor of Management from the University of Hertfordshire in 2018.

Jacqueline Janssen is a Self-employed Consultant in the Netherlands, where she collaborates in Public-Private Partnerships and practice-based research. She graduated as Doctor of Management from the University of Hertfordshire in 2016.

Robbert Masselink is an Organisational Consultant at het Zuiderlicht, a consultancy firm in the Netherlands. He is a Lecturer at the Business University of Nyenrode and a Visiting Lecturer at the University of Groningen and the University of Utrecht. Robbert graduated as Doctor of Management from the University of Hertfordshire in 2019.

Karina Solsø is a Self-employed Organisational Consultant in Denmark working with organisational change and leadership development. She is also a Visiting Lecturer at Hertfordshire Business School, University of Hertfordshire, UK. She graduated as Doctor of Management from the University of Hertfordshire in 2016.

Eric Wenzel is a Senior Partner in a globally operating HR consulting firm, where he focuses on board advisory services, such as executive coaching, top team development and transformation consulting. He graduated as Doctor of Management from the University of Hertfordshire in 2012.

PREFACE TO THE COMPLEXITY AND MANAGEMENT SERIES

THE KEY IDEAS OF COMPLEX RESPONSIVE PROCESSES OF RELATING AND THEIR RECENT DEVELOPMENT

Chris Mowles

Our experience at work tells us that we make plans but they rarely turn out as we intended. We communicate as clearly as we can, but we are still often misunderstood. Even when acting with the best of intentions we can cause harm. Sometimes, leaders and managers become brutally aware that they may be in charge, but they are not always in control because work life has the quality of being predictably unpredictable. Management training and education has become much more widespread in the last 30 years, yet still largely relies on assumptions of predictability and control. Often dealing with abstractions and idealisations, the majority management discourse rests on assumptions of an orderly world where leaders and managers propose and dispose using tools and techniques of technical rationality (Stacey, 2012).

The minority disciplines within the natural sciences, the sciences of complexity, have been an alternative source domain for thinking differently about the stable instability of organisational life for more than 30 years. Even so, management as a tradition finds it hard to shake off old habits. Just as it is now widely accepted that organisations are sites of complex activity, so there are tendencies within organisational scholarship that assume that even complexity can be managed, putting the manager back in control. For example, it may be assumed that the manager can decide whether a situation is simple, complicated or complex, thus determining whether a 'complexity approach' is needed or not. Alternatively, it may be suggested that a manager can 'unleash/embrace/encourage' complexity, as though complexity is always good and is at the manager's command, thus reinstating managerial control.

Uniquely, then, the books, articles and teaching which has emerged from the faculty group at the University of Hertfordshire (UH), and graduates of the Doctor of Management (DMan) programme there, have taken up insights from the complexity sciences, but have tried at the same time to cleave to their radical implications. It has been a decades-long experiment working with the idea that ultimately the social world is uncontrollable, but that we need to find ways to go on together anyway. This is not the same as saying that there is nothing to be done. Rather, the perspective developed at UH, termed complex responsive processes of relating, takes management seriously as a contingent group activity that requires highly reflective and reflexive individuals to negotiate and improvise, particularly in situations of high uncertainty. It assumes that some ways of managing are more helpful than others, and that with practice, it is possible to become more skilful.

Between 2000 and 2008, Routledge produced a series of volumes, both single-author and curated books of chapters written by faculty and graduates from the DMan programme, which set out this perspective. The foundational volume was the jointly authored book by Ralph Stacey, Doug Griffin and Patricia Shaw titled *Complexity and Management: Fad or Radical Challenge to Systems Thinking*. In it the authors interpreted the complexity sciences by analogy and drew on the social sciences to locate it as a resource for social science thinking and research. It marked a radical departure for organisational theory and was a pioneering attempt to mobilise complexity theory to understand organisational life. The subsequent series of edited volumes was titled *Complexity and the Experience of Organizing* and comprised titles on research, managing and leading in the public sector, emergence, improvisation, values and leadership (Stacey, 2005; Stacey and Griffin, 2005a; Stacey et al., 2000). These volumes evolved out of the research work undertaken by students on the DMan, which had become an experiential doctorate run along psychodynamic lines. The volumes had wide appeal and demonstrated the importance of taking every day complex experience seriously, inquiring into it as a participant rather than from an assumed independent position.

The current series reimagines the experience of 15 years ago with the programme under the directorship of Chris Mowles and faculty colleagues Nick Sarra, Karen Norman, Emma Crewe, Karina Solsø and Kiran Chauhan. To date, more than 70 DMan students have successfully completed their doctorates. Over recent years, the graduates in the programme have drawn on a wider and wider variety of scholars and ideas to illuminate their work, including anthropology, social psychology, political economy, feminism, intersectionality and critical organisational theory.

In these co-edited volumes (Leadership, Consultancy and Management in the public sector), the first in a new series, a group of vibrant, engaged researchers inquire into complex phenomena at work and write about the insights they have gained as a way of provoking resonance, recognition and insight in the reader. This is very different from the more orthodox entity-based research which is more typical in business schools, or research which is undertaken to increase the effectiveness or efficiency of organisations, or to test some tool or technique of management. Rather, the research in this volume is driven by doubt and curiosity to draw out the plurality of everyday interactions in organisations. Aimed at producing complex knowledge, it is governed simply by paying attention to what is going on and what sense people are making of it, including the researcher. The generalisability of the findings, their usefulness if you like, is to be found in the extent to which the reader finds this resonant, provoking, insightful and wise. There are no tools, techniques of stepwise methods to be found here.

Readers of the original Routledge series may be interested in comparing and contrasting methods and references from the previous publications to judge how thinking has changed. But first it is worth going back over some of the original scholarship which shaped the thinking of the founding of the DMan and the perspective it embodied, which I do briefly now as a way of providing some context for the chapters which follow. This review does not do justice to the wide variety of sources which students and graduates now draw on for their research, but it may help frame the key tenets of thinking which pervade the chapters in this volume.

Theoretical and practical origins

At the beginning of the millennium, three colleagues at the UH, Ralph Stacey, Doug Griffin and Patricia Shaw, decided to start a new professional doctorate. The trio's aim was to combine all that was productive, if sometimes uncomfortable, from their shared experience of group-based pedagogy with an interdisciplinary research perspective combining the natural and social sciences. This perspective was forged in a very close friendship between the three colleagues, a fact consonant with the perspective they were developing, and which highlights the centrality of relationships to understanding social life.

Starting the DMan also marked a theoretical break from Stacey's previous oeuvre and fascination with the complexity sciences. Ralph had been working with researchers in groups for some time, but in his previous publications he had argued that organisations were complex adaptive systems (CAS), or that they were like them, using the complexity sciences as metaphor. CAS are computer-based models comprising multiple interacting agents. He even argued that complexity thinking was applied in certain situations and not others, the subject of the still ubiquitous Stacey diagram.[1] After many heated hours of discussion, Stacey, Griffin and Shaw moved from simple metaphor to interpret the CAS by analogy, identifying properties of interest in the models and refracting them to the social domain. In doing so they tried to hang on to the generative tension of keeping an in-depth understanding of CAS to set alongside a granular interpretation of relevant social theory, and argued that complexity applies in all situations and at all degrees of scale.

I explore what the two domains share in common, and what the conceptual implications are later. But the combined perspective these colleagues developed, complex responsive processes of relating, is an example of what the French philosopher Edgar Morin (2005) later expressed as a necessary development in dealing with insights from the complexity sciences. Morin argued that there needed to be a transition from a restricted understanding of complexity to a general understanding. He set out to encourage new ways of thinking that brought the natural and social sciences together. For him, there was further to go than simply collapsing some of the radical implications of taking the complexity sciences seriously into orthodox natural science thinking based on disaggregation, prediction, and control:

> The principle of disjunction, of separation (between objects, between disciplines, between notions, between subject and object of knowledge),

should be substituted by a principle that maintains the distinction, but that tries to establish the relation.

(ibid.: 7)

Complex responsive processes of relating are an attempt at describing such a new paradigm of thinking, researching and acting which privileges relationships, process and collaboration, uniting the knower and the known in paradoxical tension.

The perspective originally wove together four principal traditions of thought: the complexity sciences, in particular evolutionary CAS, pragmatic philosophy, process sociology, especially Norbert Elias, and group analytic thinking and practice. I briefly explore these four influences sequentially. The purpose of the following paragraphs is to point to some of the key assumptions which inform the work of authors contributing to this volume, so that the reader might better locate their arguments.

Complexity – radically different assumptions about stability and change

More orthodox theories of management often contain assumptions about social life drawing on systems theory, which depend on spatial metaphors, notions of equilibrium, and consider organisations as entities. Organisations are described as operating at different 'levels', are disaggregated into parts and whole and go through distinct and managed processes of change. There is an assumption that managers are somehow outside the organisation understood as a system and can therefore operate upon it. As an example, in every day ways of talking about organisations, managers are thought to be able to 'move it in the right direction', to 'create the right culture', and to 'drive change'. These assumptions hide in plain sight: they are taken for granted and are therefore often not alluded to or justified, because they are dominant assumptions. This is the way that ideology works. When I present complexity ideas to groups of managers, they often rightly ask me to work hard to justify them, often without acknowledging that their own ideas about stability and change in organisations are informed by a set of ideas which are equally questionable.

The perspective of complex responsive processes of relating interprets CAS in particular as having profound implications for thinking about stability and change in social life. For example, CAS models are never at rest, but iterate, then reiterate. The implication by analogy is that this is equally true for social life. Assuming this problematises more orthodox theories of management, which propose that organisations have to undergo periods of change from an undesired stable state to an ideal stable state, stability is contrasted with change. Instead, to corrupt Churchill's observation about history, from a complexity perspective we might think that organising is simply one damned thing after another. Even states of stability are dynamically maintained.

Second, in CAS, population-wide patterns of stable-instability arise as a result of what all agents are doing together in their local interactions, and may change as a result of the amplification of small differences. Cause and effect are in a non-linear relationship. Interpreting this characteristic by analogy challenges thinking about wholesale, often top-down change predicated on linear cause and effect. To transpose this insight to organisations is to assume that whatever happens does so as a combination of managerial framing and employee interpretation in local interactions, which, in turn, feeds managerial framing. As an example, and to give a complexity perspective on why wholesale organisational change programmes often fail, what everyone is doing together in their local interactions may be precisely to resist the proposed change.

In CAS, agents negotiate conflicting constraints in their local interactions. By analogy, this directs us to think about how people in organisations negotiate their mutual constraints, their power relationships at work. Power and politics are often avoided in contemporary organisations and orthodox organisational scholarship, and when they are we avoid the ethical implications of the negotiation of how to go on together. Fourth, in CAS there is no controlling agent or group of agents which direct activity. Interpreting this characteristic by analogy deflates the common assumption that individual leadership is everything. Thinking about general patterns of influence is not the same as denying the importance of leaders, but rather broadens our thinking to consider the exercise of authority as an improvisational group activity.

And last, CAS have a paradoxical movement: local interaction creates the global pattern, while at the same time the global pattern shapes local activity. In organisational life, we can only take up idealisations of global patterns, call them strategies, in local activity. At the same time, our local improvisations produce what we might think of as strategy in practice. In every day management thinking, contradictions are resolved by splitting them out with the manager able to choose one pole over the other, leaders or followers, transformation or transaction, strategy or implementation. Interpreting insights from the complexity sciences from a complex responsive process perspective implies that there is no splitting and no choosing, and so no escaping the paradox.

Evolutionary CAS interpreted by analogy do offer a different source domain for thinking about what's going on when we're at work trying to get things done with other people. But they only take us so far, and are, after all, models which run on computers. In order to develop a more subtle, durable suite of ideas, in a move from a restricted to a general understanding of complexity, complex responsive processes drew on three additional strands of thinking from the social sciences/humanities. In doing so it sketched out a more comprehensive theory of mind, of action, of identity, of communication, of ethics and of the paradox of stability and change.

Pragmatic philosophy

Complex responsive processes of relating are infused with pragmatic thinking. Pragmatic philosophy, particularly the works of GH Mead (1932/2002, 1934), John Dewey (1929/2008, 1946), and Dewey and Bentley (1949), directs us to consider the importance of everyday experience. We mobilise our human capacity for doubt, the ability to reflect on what we are doing. If, as the CAS suggest, global patterns arise simply and only from what we are all doing together acting locally, then the pragmatists' preoccupation with experience, which turns on the exploration of what we are doing together and what sense we make of it, is a useful perspective. Rather than proceeding from abstract ideas, from the idea of systems, pragmatism is concerned with what people are saying and doing in the co-construction of their social worlds. Both Mead and Dewey assume a thoroughly social self, that the body is in the social world and the social world is in the body. We are formed by the social world, just as we form it, the same dynamic of forming and being formed that I drew attention to in CAS.

The perspective of complex responsive processes of relating draws on Mead's complex theory of communication, that in order to understand each other we communicate in shared significant symbols. Equally the perspective borrows his idea about the predictable unpredictability of conversation, that meaning arises in our gestures towards one another taken together with the responses these provoke, both in ourselves and in others.

We may start out by knowing what it is we want to say but change our minds as we hear ourselves speaking and as we notice and respond to our interlocutors. Consonant with Morin's suggestion that we consider the subject and object of knowledge in relation, so pragmatism works to overcome dualisms, self and other, I, me, and we, and reframes them as paradoxes. Both Dewey and Mead were concerned with an emergent theory of ethics which addresses the competing goods in any dynamic situation.

Process sociology

The main sociological informant of the original statement of complex responsive processes of relating is Norbert Elias (1978, 2000, 2001), who also considers the 'I' and 'we' element of our personality structures to be two sides of the same coin. For Elias, the relatively contemporary idea that we are discrete, autonomous individuals cut off from one another is an illusion which doesn't serve us well. Instead, we are highly interdependent, social selves with no 'inside' and no 'outside', just as there is no outside of social life from which we gain a privileged view. Elias frames the structure/agency discussion at the heart of sociology as a paradox: society is made up of highly social individuals who together create the *habitus*, the dynamic recognisable patterns of behaviour which we shape and which shape us. Our place in the social network we are born into and the groups we belong to produces our sense of self: paradoxically it individualises us. I argue that this is a shared assumption between Mead, Dewey, and Elias, and is consonant with the interpretation I made from CAS previously.

Though Elias developed his oeuvre long before there were computers, he develops similar insights about society that I drew by interpretation from CAS. Elias is preoccupied by the fact that language and thinking represents entities at rest much better than it does relationships in motion. Instead, he uses the analogy of the game both to understand the constant change in social life and to frame the role of power and reflective detachment in gaining social advantage. We are interdependent and have need of one another: the greater the need, the greater the power disadvantage. But so too greater power accrues to those who are able to notice their own participation in the game of social life. This too is resonant with the value that Dewey in particular attributes to our human capacity for reflection and thought in the deepening of experience.

Group analytic theory

SH Foulkes, the founder of group analytic theory and practice (1964/2002; Foulkes and Anthony, 1957/1984), had a troubled friendship with his fellow German Jewish refugee, Nobert Elias. Both were concerned with inherent sociality of human beings, and shared the insight that we could act more wisely if we gained insight into group dynamics and our own participation in them. For Foulkes, the best way to find out about a group was to participate in a group, so developed a method of running agendaless, free-flowing inquiry in groups, where the principal task is to talk about what is going on. This brings to mind the focus of the pragmatists and their interest in what it is we are doing together and how we come to think and talk about it. In the course of inquiry a variety of perspectives emerge: there is no need for consensus and no need to take action, except the action of noticing and reflecting. The point is to be together with no particular end in view and to pay attention to relationships. Foulkes called this the development of 'group mindedness', which we might understand as a form of decentring of the self, or reflexivity.

Experiential groups run in the tradition of Foulkesian thinking are at the heart of the method adopted by the DMan, and every graduate of the programme will have experienced a minimum of 36 one-and-a-half-hour group meetings run without anyone in charge and without a task except to talk about what the participants have on their minds.

Summary: key ideas which inform the chapters in this volume

All four strands of intellectual tradition inform the perspective of complex responsive processes of relating privilege history, sociality, and paradox. The social theory which underpins the insights from the complexity sciences weave together the traditions of Aristotle, Hegel, and Darwin to focus on the processual and evolutionary qualities of social life.

All the chapters in this volume borrow from and develop the founding ideas of complex responsive processes and borrow from the intellectual traditions outlined above. They also supplement and deepen them with their own reading. In doing so, they take what is considered a micro-social approach to researching organisations and depend upon narrative and interpretation. The focus on everyday interaction arises from the key insight informing the perspective of complex responsive processes that whatever happens does so as a result of what everyone is doing together. As a set of intellectual assumptions, complex responsive processes are concerned with the structured flux of relationships, power, practical judgement and ethics. It is concerned to complexify our thinking about the social world, but nonetheless to draw distinctions, to generalise, to call out resonance and to provoke.

To be clear that there are no easy answers in working out how to go on together is not the same as giving up and claiming that there is nothing to be done. Rather, the emphasis in the chapters in this volume is to make sense of what the researchers have been doing in the hope of acting more wisely in future, on producing complex and plural ways of thinking more helpful in navigating uncertain times.

References

Dewey, J. (1929/2008) *The Quest for Certainty: The Later Works 1925–1953*, Vol. 4, Carbondale: Southern Illinois University Press.

Dewey, J. (1946) *The Public and Its Problems*, New York: Gateway Books.

Dewey, J. and Bentley, A. (1949) *Knowing and the Known*, Boston, MA: Beacon Press.

Elias, N. (1978) *What is Sociology?*, London: Hutchinson and Co.

Elias, N. (2000) *The Civilising Process: Sociogenetic and Psychogenetic Investigations*, Oxford: Blackwell.

Elias, N. (2001) *The Society of Individuals*, London: Continuum Books.

Foulkes, S.H. (1964/2002) *Therapeutic Group Analysis*, London: Karnac Book.

Foulkes, S.H. and Anthony, E.J. (1957/1984) *Group Psychotherapy: The Psychoanalytic Approach*, London: Karnac Books.

Mead, G.H. (1932/2002) *The Philosophy of the Present*, New York: Prometheus Books.

Mead, G.H. (1934) *Mind, Self and Society from the Standpoint of a Social Behaviourist*, Chicago, IL: University of Chicago Press.

Morin, E. (2005) Restricted complexity, general complexity. Presented at the Colloquium "Intelligence de la complexite: "epistemologie et pragmatique", Cerisy- La- Salle, France, June 26th, 2005". Translated from French by Carlos Gershenson.

ACKNOWLEDGEMENTS

This book is dedicated to the memory of Ralph Stacey and the remarkable community he helped to create at the University of Hertfordshire through the Doctor of Management programme.

Ralph was always interested in the dilemmas experienced by consultants and took a lively and thoughtful interest in the work of his students.

He took pleasure in getting behind the surface of things and enjoyed expressing his exasperation at the excesses of instrumental managerialist tendencies so familiar in contemporary organisational life. He was kindly, humorous and at times extremely fierce in his approach and always very determined.

The writers of this volume were all Ralph's students and are members of a wider community of practice which extends beyond their doctoral work and without which Ralph's own work could not have developed. He would have been delighted with their achievements.

The community he helped to found along with Patricia Shaw and Doug Griffin works together to continually develop understanding about organisational life and the contributions here are indebted to a participation in countless conversations and readings about actual events which go on in the day-to-day work of the students on the programme as well as with and between the faculty lead by Chris Mowles and which, besides Karina and

Nick, include Karen Norman, Kiran Chauhan, and Emma Crewe, all of whom bring specific skills and experience and a capacity to develop ideas in an ongoing way.

Most of the writers in this volume came through a particular learning set on the Doctor of Management programme and together conducted research into the particular themes in consultancy explored through these pages. So, besides the writers included here, it's important to acknowledge the contributions over the years of Luke Mkubvu, Sam Talucci, Pradeep Sharma, Asa Lundquist Coey, Majken Askeland, Michal Goldstein, Carla Blackadder, Svein Hoftun, and Rebecca Myers, all of whom helped to develop the work here.

Finally, but certainly not least, to our partners Bryony and Jonas for their endless patience, encouragement, love, and support.

Note

1 Stacey abandoned the diagram when he accepted that complexity wasn't a special condition that applied in certain circumstances but is a quality of all human relating. Additionally, he was concerned that such diagrams, which are ubiquitous in business schools, give false reassurance that managers are still in control.

INTRODUCTION

Karina Solsø and Nicholas Sarra

This book explores the complexity and uncertainty of consultancy practice. The consultancy experience is presented here in a rigorous and nuanced manner, which tries to give a granular account of consultancy practice as opposed to some idealised view or prescriptions of what should be happening.

Each chapter involves autoethnographic narrative descriptions of the messy and complex nature of consultancy work including the doubts and uncertainties that permeate the everyday lives of consultants. In each of the chapters, this sense of doubt and uncertainty become the starting point of reflective inquiry and theorising. As such, the unique contribution of this book lies in the thickness of narrative descriptions as well as in critical and reflexive theorising, which offers novel and thought-provoking ideas about their practice. As editors of this book, we suggest that contributions of this kind are important in the field of consultancy literature, because of their difference from many publications in the field which take a prescriptive and instrumental view which tends to conceal the complex, political and emotionally embodied nature of consultancy practice.

Recently, there has been some discussion about whether there is a sense of stagnation in the Organisation Development (OD) tradition. Critique has been raised within this tradition that there haven't been any serious innovations since the emergence of Appreciative Inquiry back in 1987 (Cameron, 2020). This critique has once again restarted a debate amongst OD researchers about 'the rigour-relevance balance', with researchers emphasizing rigour whilst practitioners ask for relevance (Paine & Delmhorst, 2020). The problem which has been repeatedly articulated is that practitioners don't seem to find the research particularly helpful, because the research tends to be too disconnected from practice. Researchers coming from different traditions have different solutions to this problem. For example, Cummings and Cummings (2020) argue that the most promising way forward is through relying more extensively on action research as an approach to knowledge creation. Cameron (2020) finds hope in 'Positive Organizational Scholarship', which "aims to reveal and foster positive capabilities and activities that lead to flourishing in organizations". Beer (2020) emphasizes the collaboration between researchers and practitioners in creating actionable knowledge with clarity around why, when and how new practices improve organizational outcomes. Beer's apparent longing for a stronger sense of explanatory causal connection between interventions and their outcomes can be seen to reflect a more general trend around instrumentality in OD research.

A key assumption underpinning OD research is that the key task is to seek causal explanations of organizational phenomena. The validity of this knowledge "rests on its ability to explain organizational phenomena; the validity of OD knowledge is based on its effectiveness in guiding action in a valued direction" (Cummings & Cummings, 2020).

Attempts to guide the actions of OD practitioners in a valuable direction developed from Action Research (Lewin, 1947) and the T-group (Lippitt & Lippitt, 1978), followed by Schein's (1987) description of Process Consultation. Later, the tradition developed to include a focus on Organisational Learning (Argyris & Schön, 1978, 1996) and Teambuilding (Tannenbaum et al., 1992). The most recent branches of the OD tree show the influence of the social constructionist discourse with Appreciative Inquiry (Cooperrider & Srivastva, 1987; Gergen, 2009) as well as the development of Dialogic OD (Busche & Marshak, 2009, 2015).

Each of these theories has attempted to fulfil the research task of seeking explanations of organizational phenomena; each of these theories attempts at creating value through guiding actions in directions that create value.

From the perspective of the chapters comprising this book, we wonder about whether this focus on 'guiding actions in directions that create value' can potentially be counterproductive. Most literature on consultancy shares two characteristics, which can be seen to arise out of this particular understanding of the task and the value of OD research: (1) It is focused on tools and techniques – instruments by which the consultant can help groups of people develop and change (Mowles, 2011), and (2) it often portrays organisational life and consultancy practices in idealised ways which neglect, suppress or marginalize more uncomfortable aspects of experience. The implication of this is that consultants may struggle to find resonance in the above theoretical descriptions. The complexity and uncertainty of everyday consultancy life is out of tune with the clarity and orderliness implicit in the literature. In the following, we reflect on these two characteristics in order for us to present an alternative view that is offered by the chapters within this book.

Tools and instrumentalism in OD

The use of tools is a significant human capacity, without which we wouldn't be able to do much (Byrne, 1995). Tools are artefacts that we use to increase and extend our human capacities. Through the use of tools, we regulate our human activity and enable the realization of our goals (Stacey, 2012). Tools are seen to play a significant role in most of the OD literature. Here, organisations are seen as self-regulating systems and the consultant is seen as a detached observer, who – through tools-based analysis and intervention – can help groups of people bring about the desired change (Mowles, 2011). There is an implicit assumption that these tools make it possible for the consultant to choose and control the future of the organisation to some degree. As such, relying on tools involves some degree of instrumental rationality. If a consultant uses a tool in a proper way, then the desired outcome will materialise (Stacey, 2012). Being competent as a consultant is largely seen as being aware of and confident with a variety of tools and capable of using them flexibly.

According to Stacey (ibid.), tools can be seen as *second-order abstractions*. Abstractions are attempts to describe and make sense of the generalised patterns that we are caught up in when we interact with others. First order abstractions are our stories about our experience. Stories are abstractions because they involve simplification and interpretation of our embodied experience. Second-order abstractions involve yet another move away from embodied experience through further simplification. In management and consultancy literature, this often takes the form of either 2×2 grids or by stages which follow each other in a chronological form. The advantage of tools is the clarity and uniformity through which consultancy can be practiced; they enable the possibility of feeling a degree of control. This sense of control may mitigate the overwhelming uncertainty and attendant anxiety that sometimes comes together with the responsibility of consultants.

One of the ways in which tools offer a sense of control for consultants (and their clients) is through establishing a sense of linearity when it comes to time. The earliest example in OD, perhaps, is Lewin's unfreeze-move-freeze model (Lewin, 1947), which has been powerful in practitioners' ways of thinking about change. A more recent example is the 4D model of Appreciative Inquiry (Cooperrider & Srivastva, 1987), a tool which is being used to plan change processes, by ordering the change into managed stages. These tools have the advantage of helping consultants order their practice and interventions. They provide consultants with a discourse by which they can talk about the change with a sense of clarity and confidence. The complex change that nobody can really manage in their minds becomes manageable through these tools and models. Furthermore, the use of tools may be seen as serving to decontextualize the politics of the consultancy encounter, rendering them invisible and masking the improvisatory gestures of participants and consultants alike. This instrumentalising and categorising of the world renders problematic the notion of human freedom as Solsø, drawing upon Arendt (1958) and Loidolt (2019), points our attention to in Chapter 4; for if consultancy method is deterministic as to outcome, then participants are reduced to automata without ethical choice. Technical responsibilities come to take precedence over moral responsibilities or obscure them entirely.

The chapters comprising this book involve a reflective scepticism about the way tools often get used in consultancy practice. This is not a question about using tools or not. Certainly, to be included in the groups of consultants who are hired to do work, one has to be a skilled participant in this discourse (Stacey, 2012). However, being reflexive about the responses of others and oneself when these tools are in use is key when it comes to both being effective as a consultant and also in the context of the moral aspects of consultancy practice.

In Chapter 1, Chauhan uses an example of working with *Open Space Technology* to explore the way in which the practice of consultants is shaped by the mutual expectations about what a consultant ought to do in particular situations. The expectations towards the consultant are partly shaped by the tools the consultant chooses to use, and as such the tools play a significant function in regulating the actions and expectations of participants. The tools enable action, but at the same time, tools play a powerful role in closing down spaces for further inquiry, which may be significant in the context of change. Chauhan demonstrates how tools perform a function through the ordering and categorising of a context of uncertainty. He also demonstrates how this ordering and categorising can lead to a collapse of the space within which it is possible to think in nuanced ways about what is going on and the moral significance of the situation.

A key limitation of consultancy tools therefore lies in the inconsistency between the certainty and clarity of the tool and the uncertainty and messiness of social interaction. The complexity of social interaction will inevitably exceed the clarity and uniformity of the tool, which can easily be experienced as a loss of control, particularly if the participants in a group expect the consultant to be in control and manage a change process according to a particular tool. If the simplifying logic of tools comes to dominate the expectations towards consultants, leaving everyone with an illusion of certainty and predictability, then the capacity of everyone to actually respond to the unique openings that arise in the emergent conversation may collapse. This collapse can have moral consequences, as well as implications for the capacity for novelty to arise (Mowles, 2011; Stacey, 2012).

A number of authors in the book mention their emotional or affectual responses as central to their understanding of the consultancy situation. The sense of collapse referred to above is mitigated through reflexivity into the emotionally nuanced context of consultancy. In the literature on emotion in organisational studies, authors often distinguish between emotion and affect, where emotion refers to the ways in which psychobiologists approach emotions through a positivistic framework to find universal phenomena across a variety of contexts and situations (Wetherell, 2012); an approach that has been critiqued for the tendency to sanitize and scientize the phenomenon of emotion into a physiological sensation (Townley, 2008). Affect, on the other hand, is taken up by scholars to resist the tendency towards reification and process reduction. Wetherell (2012) draws attention to *affective practices*, which:

> focus on the emotional as it appears in social life and tries to follow what participants do. It finds shifting, flexible and often over-determined figurations rather than simple lines of causation, character types and neat emotion categories.
>
> (ibid, p. 4)

In this book, authors don't distinguish between emotion and affect, and both of these terms are understood in a way that is similar to what Wetherell describes when using the concept of affect. It means embodied meaning-making, and emotion is a means of knowing the world, as a visceral apprehension of context. The consultant's emotional response resonates with the complex histories of their unique life and intergenerational experience. In this sense, emotion becomes our means to make sense in the moment, through our condensed and undifferentiated experience, of all moments and the anticipation of all moments to come. Through emotion, the implications of the present are imbued in the moment with the experiences of the past and the anticipations of the future (Shaw, 2002). This apprehension of the moment through emotional response is, of course, fallible; we can only rely on our historically evolved capacities to experience and to interpret those experiences, and thus, we have to remain open to ongoing reinterpretation (Bernstein, 2007). The current context may be novel in some respects in relation to our previous experience. So, the consultant's ways of responding to given situations are formed through their histories of responding to other individuals and groups, which may prove to be more or less relevant but have the potential to open us to a vast array of historical experience. Nonetheless, experiencing breakdowns and in unique moments in time stir up emotion, which allows consultants like Chauhan and Curtis to make some sense of their feelings of shame, for example, as a signal for potential exclusion from significant groups. Therefore, emotion informs agency and through reflexivity we gain the potential to move beyond flight/fight responses or compulsive reaction to existential threat.

This book holds the perspective that possibilities for skilful and insightful action are more likely to arise if groups can manage to stay with the feelings evoked by uncertainty for a little longer than usual rather than hankering after solution finding, which can amount to little more than anxiety alleviation. Often, when uncertainty is a felt quality in a conversation, a strong pressure on the consultant is co-created in a social setting with the purpose of alleviating the uncertainty, for example, through the consultant introducing the next step within the logic of the model or the tool. In moments of uncertainty, consultants often have a lively – sometimes hectic – private conversation about how to respond. The urge from participants as well as the temptation coming from within one's own need for control can lead to a collapse of the inquiry. The temptation becomes one of going along with the tool that offers a route in a landscape, which is already complex and demanding. This dilemma is discussed by Wenzel in Chapter 3 where he explores people's needs for their identities to be affirmed through paradoxical processes of recognition and misrecognition and by Solsø in her description of what can be achieved through focussing upon the politics of participation.

We are interested in the potential for change that can emerge when a group of people can manage to stay with the heat of this uncertainty. That is when the doubt and the questions that arise from conversational inquiry into the lived experience of change for the people involved can be dwelled upon in a way that can allow for an exploration of the emergent themes arising in the conversation in the living present. Although they may wish to do so, people cannot reinvent themselves instantly or convincingly in terms of their performed identities (Goffman, 1969). We are pattern creating creatures who constrain and enable ourselves, to express through our interactions, our habitual power relationships (Elias, 1991). This means that the emergent interaction of the consultancy situation tends to express whatever relational patterns are current for the group present. The consultant is therefore inevitably co-opted into the interdisciplinary processes which construct these relational patterns. The sense of uncertainty, which many consultants are prone to wish to alleviate, may herald the expressive breaking through into open communication of habituated patterns of relating which may have masked uncomfortable political difficulties. This tolerance of uncertainty by the consultant therefore creates an opportunity, not without its own risks, of permitting an engagement with underlying dynamics which may create new possibilities for people present.

Consultancy which attends closely to the dynamics of conversation is not about learning a new tool. It takes seriously the process of reflexivity about one's own participation. It means practicing one's capacity to exercise judgment critically and reflexively whilst improvising in an ever-changing political landscape together with others.

Such a process involves confrontations with one's own contingencies and patterns of interaction. These confrontations with oneself can be painful, and can easily lead to feelings of incompetence or inadequacy, particularly if these themes are organising the emotional worlds of other participants. The chapters within this book explore consultancy experiences of inadequacy, shame, guilt, powerlessness and feelings of incompetence. Such experiences are familiar to those participating in organisations and worth exploring as inevitable qualities in many consultancy encounters.

Idealised portraits of reality – the neglect, invisibility and marginalization of uncomfortable aspects of experience

In their summary of the OD tradition, Cheung-Judge and Holbeche (2015) summarize 'the OD core values' as (1) democracy and participation, (2) openness to lifelong learning and experimentation, (3) equity and fairness – the worth of every individual, (4) valid information and informed choice and (5) enduring respect for the human side of enterprise. According to Cheung-Judge and Holbeche, the early founders saw these values as 'practice values', and they believed that "these values, when operating effectively, would engage people collaboratively to address a wide range of organization issues, as well as help organizations to search for lasting solutions to incredible challenges in the changing world" (ibid, p. 19).

The most recent OD innovations, namely Appreciative Inquiry (Cooperrider & Srivastca, 1987) and Dialogic OD (Busche & Marshak, 2015), are very explicit about their idealisation around appreciation and dialogue. According to Cooperrider:

> Appreciation is creative rather than conservative precisely because it allows itself to be energized and inspired by the voice of mystery. As an active process of valuing the factors that give rise to the life-enhancing organisation, appreciation has room for the vital uncertainty, the indeterminacy that is the trademark of something alive.
>
> (Cooperrider, 2001, p. 18)

Ideals of appreciation, creativity, energy, life enhancement and liveliness all have positive connotations and invite the impression of a sense of harmonious collaborative atmosphere. Likewise, in writing about dialogic practices, Cheung-Judge and Holbeche (2015) write:

> When we use dialogic practices to engage the people of a system in conversations that address their own issues, we not only solve the immediate problem, we leave behind a more evolved system, with a greater sense of direction and hopefully of personal connection, and the energy and will to work across previously unbridgeable boundaries.
>
> (ibid, p. 44)

Again, ideals like dialogue, direction, personal connection and 'energy and will to work across previously unbridgeable boundaries' are values that are very similar to the appreciative idealisations of collaboration and harmony. Such an implied refutation of the unappreciative, conflictual and critical is taken up in Masselink's chapter where he explores a nuanced view of collaboration as inherently conflictual due to the ongoing negotiations of power and difference in the consultancy situation.

The style of writing exemplified by writers like Cooperrider can be characterised as visionary and has the quality of engaging people emotionally and appeals to a yearning for a form of psychological fulfilment (Mowles, 2011, p. 118). However, visionary speak and text also have disciplinary power, and appeals to ideals can easily have the consequence of evoking guilt, shame and the potential for exclusion (Willmott, 1993, 2003) when such ideas are not realised in practice; they can become a way of covering over dissent, conflict or power struggle (Mowles, 2011).

The American social psychologist George Herbert Mead (1934), whose work informs several of the chapters in this book, thought about such ideals as cult values. Cult values are collective idealisations that arise in groups in intense social situations. In such situations, one can experience an imagined wholeness, which leaves one with a feeling of an enlarged personality. Cult values according to Mead are a very important part of our heritage. However, Mead doesn't talk about a conflict-free form of living together. The imagined wholeness exists only in the abstract. As soon as cult values are carried out – or functionalised, as Mead would have it – in concrete social interaction between people, conflict arises, because people have diverse expectations about what an ideal means in practice or because competing ideals vie against each other. Interaction between people in the workplace is an interaction between individuals with unique histories, who nevertheless can recognise their similarities and cultural affinities but which are nonetheless involved in a complex ongoing negotiation of unique perspectives and alliances of perspective. The basis of Mead's thinking is that conflict, disagreement and dissent are unavoidable aspects of our everyday experience as humans. They are aspects which can lead to feelings of guilt, shame and exclusion. These are affectual responses, which are bound to materialise in complex social situations like consulting, but which are often neglected, suppressed or marginalised in the literature on consultancy. There is often the assumption that uncomfortable experiences indicate an unhelpful situation, which somehow is not working, and that if participants in the consultancy experience are feeling good and are comfortable within that experience, then things are going well and that the comfortable experience is an outcome in itself. But what if the opposite was sometimes the case? What if the capacity for reflexivity, the development of possibility, the finding of novel direction was made possible through the disturbance of the status quo and a disruption of the accustomed patterning of power in particular groups? Then this rupturing of what we come to expect may become a sine qua non for the development of creative outcome. Here the voice of the consultant may come to play a significant role in the noticing of what might be being co-created through the emergent interaction of the participants. This suggests an attention to a different form of temporality, one focused not upon idealised futures and places we need to get to, but upon the co-creation of those futures through interaction in the living present.

A key characteristic of the chapters within this book is that they pay attention to the patterns of interaction that unfold when values and ideals are enacted in practice. In Chapter 5, Masselink draws attention to ideological notions of collaboration and the depoliticizing qualities of the ways in which collaboration is taken up in organisations, making it hard to handle agonistic aspects of collaboration. According to Masselink, drawing on the work of Georg Herbert Mead (1934), agonistic qualities are inherent aspects of collaboration, which don't disappear just because they are marginalised from the literature on organisational processes and the tools and recommendations to consultants. Likewise, Janssen in Chapter 6 looks at the implications of the dominance of abstract and idealised text and talk, which present 'glossy' images of both corporate and personal identity, leaving an affectual impact on the self and fostering feelings of alienation.

The chapters in this book don't attempt to arrive at prescriptions for what consultants should do to be successful by helping groups of people get to a desired promised land. Instead, they focus upon the reality of the lived experience of consultancy. Plurality is an essential part of the human condition (Arendt, 1958), and it is because of the fact that we are different that novelty can arise (Stacey & Mowles, 2016). Rather than developing descriptions about how to make conflict go away, this book is an example of consultants paying attention to what they are doing in their practice.

Rather than reinforcing the utopian longing for conflict-free and harmonious forms of interaction, this book acknowledges the inherent plurality of human interaction, and the chapters all wrestle with the important question of how we respond to conflict. Bernstein (2007), writing from a pragmatic position, acknowledges the struggle of engaging with a plurality of views. According to him, "The *achievement* of a 'we' – where 'we' are locked in argument with others – is a fragile and temporary achievement that can always be ruptured by unexpected contingencies" (pp. 336–337). Through engaging in reflective inquiry into the attempts at achieving such a 'we' in interaction with clients, the authors in this book produce wider and deeper understanding of that practice, which may have generalisable qualities to the practice of others. The aim of this book is not to narrow thinking in particular (positive) directions, but to provide descriptions of consultancy practice, which can allow us to understand more with an acceptance that understanding is a process which has no totality. The difficulty with idealised decontextualization of practice is that they may create such totalities of understanding. There is always more to be understood due to the movement of time and the consequent dynamism of cultures.

Recurring themes arising across the chapters

This book comprises six chapters which have a particular sequence. The first two by Chauhan and Curtis take up the experiences of internal consultants faced with the implementation of expected organisational methods. Chauhan uses Owen's Open Space Technology and Curtis, somewhat reluctantly, Myers-Briggs type processes. Both encounter difficulties along the way and both take up the experience of the consultant's experience of shame as meaningful and worthy of exploration. Chauhan questions the idea of the consultant's neutrality, suggesting that it implies a pressure to abdicate moral agency. He reengages with this problematic negation of ethics by paying close attention to his experiences of shame in the situation. For Chauhan, shame may indicate a crisis of belonging to a significant group, the potentiality of exclusion is an emotional experience which through reflexivity offers further possibilities for understanding and therefore acting with moral agency. Curtis also attends to the theme of moral agency using Mead's concept of the social object. This could be thought about as the implicit attitudinal dispositions and expectations which allow people to take an understood means of relating to a given idea. With this in mind, he explores facilitation as a social object, pointing out the pressures on the consultant to collude with an idea of facilitation which closes down and reduces the politics of team working and renders the consultant powerless and without opinion.

The following three writers explore external consultancy situations, developing a close attention to the politics of the situations described and the significance of the impasses experienced.

Wenzel in Chapter 3 focusses his attention on processes of recognition and in particular the importance of how the consultant works with their experience of being misrecognized, a quality which may arise when, as is often the case, things do not go according to plan. He explores the possibilities which arise when the consultant can tolerate the anxiety and even anger of clients whose expectations are not immediately fulfilled. Implicit in his method, as with many of the writers in this volume, is an attention to the freedom of the consultant in these situations and how that freedom is enabled and constrained by those for whom he is consulting to.

In Chapter 4, Solsø explicitly takes up issues of freedom and meaningfulness for both consultant and participants and the significance of taking seriously the interpersonal politics of consultancy in work cultures in which instrumental rationalities and a preoccupation with outcome and productivity tend to negate this sense of freedom and meaningfulness. This emphasis on procedures and outcomes may lead to hopelessness and a sense of impasse for those involved since differences become buried or concealed. Drawing upon Arendt, Solsø uses the idea of actualising plurality as a means of creating real movement in a tense consultancy situation.

In his chapter, Masselink takes up the complexity of collaboration and in particular the agonistic and conflictual aspects of collaboration in the consultancy endeavour. Like other writers in this volume, Masselink demonstrates the importance of reflexivity into the embodied emotional experience of the consultant as a means of engagement with the situation to hand. In his view, the idealisation of collaboration conceals the paradoxical nature of the process, which again is an engagement, often fraught with relational difficulty, with the politics of difference.

Finally, Janssen turns the tables and writes about her experience of being coached on how to market herself on seeking to return to the world of work. Her experience on her sense of self, informed through insights from her own practice as a consultant, of being on the receiving end of a particular style of consultancy, exposes the perils of such processes. The pressure to embody and perform an idealised self threatens to reduce her to a branded corporate artefact.

References

Arendt, H. (1958). *The Human Condition.* Chicago, IL: University of Chicago Press.

Argyris, C. & Schön, D. A. (1978). *Organizational Learning.* Reading, MA: Addison-Wesley.

Argyris, C. & Schön, D. A. (1996). *Organizational Learning II: Theory, Method, and Practice.* Reading, MA: Addison-Wesley.

Beer, M. (2020). Making a Difference: Developing Actionable Knowledge for Practice and Theory. *Journal of Applied Behavioral Science*, 56(4), 495–509.

Bernstein, R. J. (2007). *The New Constellation.* Cambridge: Polity Press.

Busche, G. R. & Marshak, R. J. (2009). Revisioning Organization Development: Diagnostic and Dialogic Premises and Patterns of Practice. *Journal of Applied Behavioral Science*, 45, 348.

Busche, G. R. & Marshak, R. J. (2015). *Dialogic Organization Development: The Theory and Practice of Transformational Change.* San Francisco, CA: Berrett-Koehler Publishers.

Byrne, R. (1995). *The Thinking Ape: Evolutionary Origins of Intelligence.* Oxford: Oxford University Press.

Cameron, K. (2020). Responses to the Problem of OD Stagnation: A Tribute to Warner Burke. *The Journal of Applied Behavioral Science*, 56(4), 462–481.

Cheung-Judge, M. & Holbeche, L. (2015). *Organization Development*, 2nd ed. London: Kigan Page.

Cooperrider, D. (2001). *Positive Image, Positive Action: The Affirmative Basis of Organizing.* Stipes Publishing L.L.C. https://mitchmatthews.

com/wp-content/uploads/2021/01/06-Cooperrider-1990-Pos-Image-Pos-Action-1.pdf

Cooperrider, D. L. & Srivastva, S. (1987). Appreciative inquiry in organizational life. In W. Pasmore & E. Woodman (Eds.), *Research in Organization Change and Development* (Vol. 1, pp. 129–169). Bingley: JAI Press.

Cummings, T. G. & Cummings, C. (2020). The Relevance Challenge in Management and Organization Studies: Bringing Organization Development Back In. *The Journal of Applied Behavioral Science*, 56(4), 521–546.

Elias, N. (1991). *The Society of Individuals*. Oxford: Blackwell.

Gergen, K. (2009). *Relational Becoming: Beyond Self and Community*. Oxford: Oxford University Press.

Goffman, E. (1969). *The Presentation of Self in Everyday Life*. Harmondsworth: Penguin.

Lewin, K. (1947). Frontiers in Group Dynamics: Concept, Method and Reality in Social Science; Equilibrium and Social Change. *Human Relations*, 1(1), 5–41.

Lippitt, R. & Lippitt, G. (1978). *The Consulting Process in Action*. La Jolla, CA: University Associates.

Loidolt, S. (2019). *Phenomenology of Plurality: Hannah Arendt on Political Intersubjectivity*. London: Routledge.

Mead, G. H. (1934). *Mind, Self and Society from the Standpoint of a Social Behaviorist*. Chicago, IL: University of Chicago Press.

Mowles, C. (2011). *Rethinking Management: Radical Insights from the Complexity Sciences*. Farnham: Gower Applied Research.

Paine, J. W. & Delmhorst, F. (2020). A Balance of Rigor and Relevance: Engaged Scholarship in Organizational Change. *The Journal of Applied Behavioral Science*, 56(4), 437–461.

Schein, E. H. (1987). *Process Consultation, Vol. 2: Lessons for Managers and Consultants*. Reading, MA: Addison-Wesley.

Shaw, P. (2002). *Changing Conversations in Organisations: A Complexity Approach to Change*. Abingdon: Taylor and Francis Ltd.

Stacey, R. D. (2012). *Tools and Techniques of Leadership and Management: Meeting the Challenge of Complexity*. London: Routledge.

Stacey, R.D. & Mowles, C. (2016). *Strategic Management and Organizational Dynamics: The Challenge of Complexity*. New York: Pearson Education Limited.

Tannenbaum, S. I., Beard, R. L., & Salas, E. (1992). Team Building and Its Influence on Team Effectiveness: An Examination of Conceptual and Empirical Developments. In K. Kelley (Ed.), *Advances in Psychology, 82. Issues, Theory, and Research in Industrial/Organizational Psychology* (pp. 117–153). Amsterdam: North-Holland.

Townley, B. (2008). *Reason's Neglect: Rationality and Organising*. Oxford: Oxford University Press.

Wetherell, M. (2012). *Affect and Emotion: A New Social Science Understanding*. London: SAGE.

Willmott, H. (1993). Strength Is Ignorance, Slavery Is Freedom: Managing Culture in Modern Organizations. *Journal of Management Studies*, 30(4), 5151–552.

Willmott, H. (2003). Renewing Strength: Corporate Culture Revisited. *M@n@gement*, 6(3), 73–78.

1

MOVING BEYOND NEUTRALITY

RECOGNISING THE MORAL AGENCY OF THE CONSULTANT THROUGH REFLEXIVE INQUIRIES INTO SHAME

Kiran Chauhan[1]

Introduction

While it is increasingly acknowledged that practitioners cannot be 'outside' the groups they work with, much of the mainstream contemporary organisational consulting literature seems to suggest that practitioners' own interests can be managed out of their work with clients. It follows then that the goal of ongoing reflexive analysis would be the maintenance of some idealised position of neutrality from which consultants can help their clients. While I agree that reflexivity can be important for consultants in becoming more aware of their habits of thinking and feeling, I would like to argue that the purpose of inquiring into one's history, values and assumptions might not be simply to prevent these interests from interfering with consulting work. Rather, these inquiries may help consultants to engage with the ethical responsibilities that may arise whenever they intervene in organisations.

In the first part of this chapter, I will suggest that organisational consultants are always asserting their agency even, for example, when they are trying to prioritise the agency of others. This means that any action a consultant takes will reflect their conscious and unconscious intentions and assumptions, and affirm or evolve their identity as well as the wider social patterns in which they are involved. This challenges the idea that consultants can intervene in organisations from a position of neutrality and helps us to think about the purposes served by the notion that one can be neutral.

Then, rather than seeing practitioner reflexivity as a tool for keeping oneself 'out of the picture' and therefore potentially avoiding responsibilities that properly rest with the consultant, I suggest that reflexive inquiry may enable a richer awareness of the ways in which consultants are involved in their relationships with clients and with others. This awareness may provide both greater choice in what consultants choose to do, but also greater responsibilities for engaging with the wider range of interests that everyday situations involve. Consequently, I suggest that moving beyond neutrality increases consultants' potential for ethical judgement. These suggestions draw primarily on the understanding of social life and ethics in the work of the American pragmatist philosopher, George Herbert Mead (1863–1931).

In the second part of the chapter, I engage with the question of what it then might mean to take these responsibilities seriously. I argue that shame can be understood as an affectual response to moral criticism whenever we challenge social norms and feel at risk of exclusion from communities that are important to us. For organisational consultants charged with catalysing helpful changes in patterns of interaction in organisations, challenging social norms or encouraging others to do so is likely to be part of everyday work. In that case, consultants, perhaps more than others, can expect to experience ethical disturbances which have the character of shame. However, consultants are involved in the production and reproduction of the same population-wide patterns as are others by their membership of complex modern societies, which includes a strong tendency to avoid or to overcome shame. I argue that taking experiences of shame seriously as they arise through reflexively analysing the memberships of real or imagined communities that are at stake, can help us to understand more about the interests that are involved in a given situation. These inquiries may expand the field of our awareness, thereby increasing our potential to act ethically.

Part 1: Neutrality, reflexivity and ethical judgement
The evolution of my practice

Throughout my career as a consultant, I have always found myself being drawn to the idea that my clients' wants or needs should take priority over my own. I started working as a strategy consultant in around 2008 to a public sector still very much in the thrall of new public management and the application of private sector practices and market economics to public institutions. At that time, I was relatively new to working life and had only really encountered organisational consultants as advisers to my more senior colleagues. It seemed obvious to me that consultants' priorities should be nothing but their clients' priorities. After all, clients were paying for consultants to help them do what *they* needed to do, even if it took some work to find out exactly what those needs were, and differed significantly from the brief that the work had been commissioned against.

Perhaps in response to a narrative in the mainstream media at the time about how consultants rarely provided value for money – which continues today – I put my energy into doing the very best job I could. I worked whatever hours were needed, travelled seemingly all the time, stayed away from home, often several times a week, and sometimes sacrificed family events in favour of work. I tried hard to understand my clients' issues, come up with potential options and likely impacts, offer suggestions about how to proceed and sometimes support implementation. There was no question for me that my clients' preferences rather than my own should guide my actions, and if there was a competition over what my clients' preferences were, then it was my job to help them decide what they wanted. I seemed to have taken on an idea of neutrality that looked a lot like selflessness.

As time passed, I encountered new ways of thinking about how consultants could work with slightly more regard for themselves. This took the form of using less structured methods of engagement and focusing more on facilitation and participation. I spent more time learning about organisational consulting from books and my practice evolved from what Edgar Schein (1987) calls the *purchase of expertise model* of consulting towards his notion of *process consultation*. In process consultation, consultants provide input based on an understanding of human processes rather than the subject matter of the consultancy and help their clients learn about these processes themselves so they can solve their own problems. As I supplemented these ideas with what have come to be known as *dialogic* approaches to organisational development (OD) (e.g. Bushe and Marshak 2015), I found myself spending less time trying to figure things out myself and more time facilitating groups as *they* tried to figure things out. I believed this was a more helpful (and efficient) way to intervene in organisations.

This sense of detachment from the group's concerns was an evolution of the way that I thought consultants should be neutral: while still aiming to be helpful rather than being led solely by clients' needs or demands, now the neutrality took the form of a purposeful detachment from clients' issues so that the responsibility for the outcomes of the work sat firmly with them rather than with me. I felt inspired by what I was learning about open systems psychodynamic consulting and from hearing eminent consultants talk about how they worked with their clients as neutral guides and used themselves as instruments. Consequently, I became much more aware of the ways in which I could use my own experience as a tool to help groups think about their problems without getting involved in those problems or giving up my detached neutrality. I would try hard to empty myself of 'memory and desire' (Bion 1967), so that I could pay attention to my embodied experience as a way of understanding what might be happening and reflecting this back in service of deepening a group's understanding about its processes. I assumed that if my interventions caused disruption, then this disruption was unlikely to be *about me*, but rather signalled that there was further work the group needed to do. And generally, this seemed to work – my clients found my interventions helpful and I gained in confidence as I became used to working in these ways.

And yet, every now and then, something would happen in my consulting work that would shake me. Though I felt intellectually able to deal with these disturbances, I would find myself restless, anxious and unable to put to bed a felt sense that I had caused some kind of harm to others or perhaps even myself. Often, these events would be accompanied by feelings of shame that I would struggle to acknowledge. Nevertheless, they prompted me towards some kind of action. It was through noticing this pattern in my experience that I started to become aware that my assumption that I could be a neutral consultant – either by following my clients' needs or through purposeful detachment – left little room for a sense myself as a moral actor in my work with clients. What happened when I felt compromised? What about when I thought I might have made things worse? What should I do?

These were the questions I started to explore that led to a problematisation of the conception of neutrality.

The problem with neutrality

Processes of socialisation such as the one I am describing are worth examining because they can offer insights into how ideas such as neutrality can come to be taken for granted amongst professionals and more generally in life. Moreover, exploring these processes can help us to think about what purposes might be being served – and what might be being avoided – by the adoption of such ways of thinking. Part of the problem I am interested in here is the implied possibility of an experiential boundary that can be drawn around a client. This boundary is a means for consultants to selectively engage with different aspects of the work, a separation which enables them to imagine they are being neutral. To be clear, this is not the same as problematising a consultant's ability to look objectively at their client's organisation or to do so without changing it – in my experience, various formulations of the observer effect, for example, the Hawthorne illumination study, along with the implications of the postmodernist insight that all observations are situated in history and social relations (e.g. Denzin and Lincoln 2017) are now well accepted in the practitioner community. Rather, I am interested in the ways that even when consultants accept that their understanding of their client is informed by their own socialisation and that their mere presence changes things, they might still assume they can separate their own interests from their clients' interests in a meaningful way.

Long before the advent of postmodernism, pragmatist philosophy took up ideas of socialisation being inseparable from perception and understanding, the unpredictability of social life and the implications of these insights for identity formation and social ordering. Mead's extensive theorising about the nature of human experience in the early decades of the 20th century drew attention exactly to these processes (Mead 1923, 1925, 1934, 1938). He suggested that it was only because of the increasingly sophisticated sensitivities we develop through encounters with others in the world that we can make reasonable guesses – sometimes quite confidently – about how we and others might act. This is achieved by instinctively filling in our perceptual gaps by drawing on the aspects of our previous experience that seem relevant to the situation at hand. For the pragmatists, it is on this basis that we instinctively act.

In this way of thinking, *identity* may then helpfully be regarded as the patterns of interpreting and responding that emerge in individual experience. Further, for Mead, the affectual gesture/response structure of the private conversations we have with ourselves (which he calls 'mind') is identical to the structure of conversations we have with actual others (which he calls 'society'). *Social order* (or culture, or habitus) in that case can be regarded as the patterns of interpreting and responding that emerge when people interact with other people. This means that both identity formation and social ordering can be thought of as aspects of the same ongoing and iterative process.

On that basis, every action, including inaction, affirms or catalyses the evolution of some aspect of identity or social order according to our individual or collective inclinations towards social compliance and rebellion in each unique situation. As I will go on to argue, this way of thinking problematises the idea that the range of sensitivities that may be in play in consulting work can be so easily separated into client and other concerns to maintain a position of neutrality. So, how might we explore what interests more holistically play into the work of organisational consulting? Mead's concept of the *social object* provides a useful starting point for reaching a more complex understanding of consultancy that can help to answer this question.

Consulting as a social object

A *social object* is defined as the object of a social act 'that answers to all parts of the complex act, though these parts are found in the conduct of different individuals' (Mead 1925: 264). In other words, social objects are *evolving expectations about the differential conduct of people involved in acts that require the co-operation of two or more people, shared by the people involved in the completion of those acts*. For example, if we consider 'commercial exchange', we think of (at least) a buyer and a seller who through different but interdependent activities complete the social act of realising the value of exchangeable goods. Commercial exchange can therefore be denoted a social object. These shared expectations may arise through a variety of social encounters and, over time, can come to be shared by large numbers of people. In these cases, a common set of responses to particular stimuli become habitual for community members in relation to recognisable complex social acts (Mead 1925, 1934). Taken together, a community's most prominent social objects are therefore another way of talking about social order, and therefore also about the identities individual social actors are invited to take up as they go about trying to live and work together.

Turning to organisational consulting, it may feel quite natural to regard consulting as what consultants do, perhaps informed by their training, research or experience. And there are any number of theoretical disciplines that consultants can draw on to inform their practice – indeed, it seems that any field that claims to offer direct or analogical insights about how humans behave, can provide a foundation for thinking about what may be happening in an organisation and therefore what will help. Illustrating the diversity of these disciplines with just one example, a recent practitioner's guide summarised the theoretical roots of OD as being complexity and chaos theory, dialogical OD, social discourse theory, psychoanalytical theory, psychodynamic theory, action research, group dynamics, systems theory, change theories, appreciative inquiry and social construction theory (Cheung-Judge and Holbeche 2015: 29).

However, thinking about organisational consulting as a social object draws attention to its relationality and its temporality – to *whose* expectations about consultancy *in what contexts over time* inform consulting practices and the identities they invite. Of course, consultancy involves consultants and clients; however, from the perspective of consulting as a social object, we may also start to think about, for example, the scholars who write about consultancy in the fields noted above; or the professional regulators or consultants' referees whom clients might look to for markers of competence or track record; or consultants' supervisors who help consultants develop their practice. All these parties may participate or contribute in complex ways to the perpetuation of the expectations about consulting that are functionalised in and evolve through day-to-day consulting interactions, and then go to form further expectations about consulting.

Neutrality in these terms might then be thought of as an aspect of the social object of consulting and is similarly complex: it is an expectation shared by those involved in consulting interactions about whose interests should be prioritised, informed by the history of the field as well as the particular context in which it is functionalised. As I described earlier, my own assumptions that I should focus on my clients' concerns first and foremost came largely from how I saw consultants working with my senior colleagues before I became a consultant myself. It was perhaps also as a response to the denigration I noticed of consultants in the media. When I found myself purposefully detaching from my client's systems, my intention to help remained the same; however, I had found a different way to be neutral. Later, I would find support for this position in the literature on consultancy that I encountered, insofar as it took up neutrality with the same assumption that consultants should keep their own concerns out of their work. For example, contemporary organisation development practitioner literature often refers to *helping* as key activity (implying that help is needed) and the consulting self as an *instrument* that can be used to understand and enhance consultants' ability to do good for their clients (e.g. Seashore et al. 2004; Rainey Tolbert and Hanafin 2006; Schein 2011; Cheung-Judge 2012; Cheung-Judge and Holbeche 2015). This literature often also has a thematic focus on greater self-awareness and reflexivity as a means to being able to become more able to focus on their clients.

Consulting literature in the open systems psychodynamic tradition has a particularly rich vocabulary for describing the ways in which consultants' underacknowledged socialisation can interfere with intervening successfully in organisations. Drawing on the psychoanalytical psychotherapy literature (e.g. Wolstein 1988), *countertransference*, for instance, is a way of speaking about how consultants' own habitual ways of responding, typically established during early life, can be triggered by their client's *transferences* onto them and colour their interpretations of and responses to what is going on in the consultation. To illustrate, transference might look like a client with an underacknowledged history of rivalry with family members, experiencing unexplainable feelings of rivalry towards the consultant whom they have engaged to help them with an organisational problem. A countertransferential response might then look like the consultant, with a history of excluding themselves from situations where they had to deal with rivalry from their family members in their own childhood, feeling that they would prefer not to do the work even if they feel they would be able to help. Recent scholarship, following postmodernist lines, argues that these tendencies are unavoidable and should therefore be considered a tool for trying to understand clients more deeply (e.g. Gertler and Izod 2004). This moves away from more traditional views that saw countertransferential tendencies as something to be worked through so that they did not interfere with trying to understand the client (e.g. Czander and Eisold 2003); however, a focus on the client is maintained.

While reflecting different disciplines, these examples of approaches to organisational consulting illustrate how the consultant's affectual experience is instrumentalised in the service of clients. Of course, we can always become more aware of the ways in which our past is material to the present, which is why consultants who take the implications of socialisation seriously might choose to have supervision themselves. However, I think these examples also suggest a general inattention to the potential importance of what goes on for consultants beyond helping their clients and how these other concerns may be important to pay attention to rather than negate under the banner of neutrality.

For, if we think about consulting as a social object even more widely, then other social actors begin to appear as being relevant: what about a consultant's own managers or colleagues or a consulting firm's shareholders? What about consultants' families or dependents who might rely on their income? What about society more widely and the regard (or lack of it) shown for consultants by, for example, the mainstream media or other trade presses? After all, in the most practical terms, organisational consulting is a commercial transaction where the client pays a consultant to work on a problem they feel unable to solve on their own. People need to want to work as consultants and be able to earn a reasonable living doing so. This brings into view considerations such as career progressions, providing for one's household, contributing to the success of the consulting firm and so on. On what basis can we say that these other concerns can be separated from the work of consulting to clients, even if they are not attended to?

Here are some examples of how these competing priorities have shown up for consultants I have encountered in recent years: an independent consultant who had recently experienced a downturn in her business, noted that even though she might not feel she could be of much help to a client who had asked her to intervene on an issue, took on the work because she was concerned about being able to keep up her household. Another consultant, this time an employee of the organisation he was consulting to, took on a piece of work he felt was of little consequence and probably not a great use of resources, because it offered the opportunity to build relationships with people who might be influential in a forthcoming restructure.

Another consultant working towards promotion in a large consulting firm found himself holding back his opinions from his client on a subject he personally felt very strongly about, because he thought that his client was looking for a specific outcome from the consultancy that was incompatible with his own perspective. He felt that bringing his personal views into his work might jeopardise his reputation and career advancement in his firm.

These illustrative cases suggest how the work of consulting could usefully be considered to include aspects of experience that may not have very much at all to do with specific clients, but which may nevertheless play consciously and unconsciously into decisions about work with specific clients. This may have direct consequences for the work being undertaken or more generally: what if our consultant who took on work because she needed the money rather than feeling able to do the work inadvertently ended up making things worse for the client, but maintained that her neutrality meant the responsibility for dealing with the fallout rested with the client? What if this coloured the perception of organisational consulting more generally in the organisation and prevented help being sought when it was needed later? What if the fact that our well-regarded internal consultant was prepared to take on the piece of work he deemed inconsequential was taken as a signal by other managers in the organisation that these pieces of work were important? What if this meant that even though the consultant got what they wanted in terms of positioning themselves in the organisation, even more time was spent on the same kinds of inconsequential activity? Lastly, what if our consultant who chose not to share his personal views prevented an exploration of the client's issue that, while unpopular, may have helped the client to make a different decision? What if not sharing his perspective led to disruption in his personal life as he dealt with a sense of self-betrayal?

These are hypothetical situations I have constructed from multiple real experiences of consulting to begin to suggest how the notion of an experiential boundary that allows the consultant to separate their interests from those of their clients might come to be seen as problematic. They also suggest how the notion of helping may leave little room for the consideration of how broader personal, organisational or societal concerns can compete with more immediate client priorities and the avoidance of uncomfortable aspects of experience. This complexifies the notion of neutrality that helping informs because multiple ends are brought into view in addition to satisfying clients' needs; as I will now go on to explore, having more of these factors in view may well increase the potential for ethical judgement.

The ethics of competing goods

It seems uncontroversial to suggest that managerialism is pervasive in contemporary organisational life (Kilkauer 2013). One need only look at the latest management or human resource (HR) bestseller lists on Amazon to understand how the quest for replicable solutions that will fix organisations' problems, enhance leadership and optimise the utilisation of financial and human resources permeates not just organisational thinking, but contemporary society more widely.

Arguably, managerialism reflects a wider post-Enlightenment trend towards greater control of the world and our individual selves. It is not surprising, then, that the assumptions about predictability that underpin managerialism also show up in approaches to ethics in the normative, deontological or utilitarian traditions. Normative and deontological ethics generally seek to establish moral rules or imperatives that can be used as standards to guide action. Utilitarian ethics seek to guide actions by evaluating the usefulness of their outcomes. These ethical traditions, like managerialist interventions in organisations, rely on the results of our conduct with others being knowable in advance. And yet, it seems to me that the outcomes of our actions are rarely predictable and the possibility of things going other than to plan is always present, sometimes in surprising and disturbing ways. Here is an illustrative example from relatively early on in my use of large group methods as a consulting tool.

I was consulting to a public sector regulatory organisation about to undergo a corporate restructure. Working with two separate groups in the organisation at roughly the same time, I was due to facilitate team away days for both. One was a team of mostly younger technical specialists who worked on innovative solutions to data processing, benchmarking and visualisation whom I hadn't worked with before; the second was a team of highly experienced managers whom I had worked with before, whose jobs involved supporting organisations in regulatory failure. Both teams were naturally anxious about the upcoming restructure and both agreed that an opportunity for team members to explore their concerns in an emergent way might be useful.

I suggested using a version of Harrison Owen's Open Space Technology (OST) (Owen 1992) to both groups, as, in my experience, it enabled a less constrained and more productive conversation than more structured approaches offered. OST is an intervention that Owen developed following the observation that when the matter at hand was particularly complex, contentious and urgent, people seemed to get more out of the coffee breaks between meetings rather than the meetings themselves. OST had become rather fashionable with public sector organisations but was somewhat outside the usual activities at team away days for this organisation.

The OST process involves participants having the opportunity to organise themselves into self-selecting groups to discuss issues that they find important in relation to a framing question, rather than topics pre-decided by workshop organisers. This ostensibly disrupts habitual patterns of interacting and power relating, enables different kinds of conversations that tap into personal motivations, emphasises freedom and choice and so may lead to different kinds of action. In this case, the framing question for both groups was about how to maintain the quality of their work during the restructure. In addition, for both groups, there were conversations with the team's director, a further conversation with a steering group in which I was able to draw on my experience to assuage concerns about the process, an email before the session explaining the process inviting team members to think about what they might want to discuss when invited to offer topics and finally an away day in which the technique was attempted.

In the event, the technical group took up the invitation enthusiastically, suggested lots of topics when the opportunity arose and seemed to have productive conversations. When I worked with them again later, these conversations seemed to have led to action and this concurred with all my previous experiences of using the technique – I felt like I had helped. The other group, however, when they were invited to offer topics sat in complete silence for what seemed like an age. This was despite having participated quite willingly in similarly unstructured processes with me before. This left me feeling embarrassed, threatened and alone. Worse still, I thought that asking them to engage with their anxieties in this way might have been distressing – something I might consider as harming them in the immediate term, even if it might turn out later to have been beneficial.

So how might we explain this radically different outcome arising from the same technique, executed in the same way, in the same organisation and context, at a similar time? A further idea from Mead is helpful here. For Mead, human experience is characterised simultaneously by senses of agency and social constraint: we feel both free to act, manifest as spontaneous responses to emerging situations, at the same time as a need to conform to the social norms that afford us membership of communities that are in some way important to us. Further, these aspects of experience are paradoxically related insofar as each goes to form the other while being conceptually opposite: our awareness of our previous spontaneous responses influences our sense of social constraint, which then influences our future responses and so on. In these terms, it is the spontaneity of our responses – the way we find out what we are doing as we do it – that accounts for unpredictable novelty in experience. Further, drawing on the analogy of the butterfly effect from the complexity sciences that small changes in non-linear systems can lead to large changes in outcomes and vice versa, the interplay of the responses of multiple social actors is also unpredictable. All of this means that we can never really know what will happen when we or others act; rather, we find out what is happening as it happens (Stacey 2012).

In the example above, we might see the organisational context and timing as being constraining factors affecting both groups in similar ways and my intervention as a similar stimulus. And yet, the groups' responses were very different. Of course, there were differences between the groups as I have described, and no doubt a host of others that may have been in play that I was not aware of. If that's likely to be the case for most consulting interventions as consultants operate with partial understandings and assumptions about the groups they are working with, then on what basis can we ever imagine interventions that have worked in the past will work again?

This creates a problem for the approaches to ethics noted above that rely on the assumption that the impact of actions can be known in advance. If we take the unpredictability of social life seriously, the only meaningful locus of ethical activity is the *process of judging* (Joas 1997). Further, each judgement is unique because the competition of values about help and harm arise uniquely in each situation at hand. Mead's formulation of ethical judgement is therefore that it comprises the inherently fallible process of taking in the widest range of interests on the matter at hand and making a judgement based on all of them. This is an intentional process that may run counter to our instincts as we are required to constantly look beyond our habits of thinking and feeling to get hold of the problem at hand and the competing values it involves. Mead says:

> The only rule that an ethics can present is that an individual should rationally deal with all the values that are found in a specific problem. ... But when the immediate interests come into conflict with others we had not recognised, we tend to ignore the others and take into account only those which are immediate. The difficulty is to make ourselves recognise the other and wider interests, and then to bring them into some sort of rational relationship with the more immediate ones. There is room for mistakes, but mistakes are not sins.
> (Mead 1934: 388–389)

This way of thinking about ethics emphasises how researching the client as well as ongoing reflexive analysis that brings more of the consultant's own habits of thinking and feeling into view can both be regarded as aspects of increasing the potential for ethical judgement. Further, consideration of the multiple interests involved beyond the client's wants or needs brought into view by understanding consultancy as a social object in its widest sense suggests that the potential for ethical judgement is increased further by widening the scope of such research and reflexive analysis beyond the clients' interests alone, and therefore beyond neutrality, to make space for the consultant's own moral agency and other relevant interests. Acknowledging these wider interests may change which are to be considered 'immediate' in Mead's terms.

The final statement in the quotation above is important in this regard as it indicates one of the challenges of adopting the pragmatists' conception of ethics: 'sin' implies a judgement about action from some God's-eye view of moral happenings and untoward consequences if the sin is unrepented for. The absence of this kind of moral adjudication places the weight of responsibility on the individual for judging what to do, which I see as a step towards recognising the moral agency of the consultant. Mead suggests that the weighing of the widest possible range of interests may lead sometimes to responses that privilege the needs of the community and sometimes one's own:

> A man has to keep his self-respect, and it may be that he has to fly in the face of the whole community in preserving this self-respect. But he does

it from the point of view of what he considers a higher and better society than that which exists.

(ibid: 389)

So how might we come to recognise the consultant's own interests that are involved in but not necessarily directly related to their work with clients, especially when the stakes are high? Put another way, how might consultants balance respect for others and respect for themselves when they feel the pressure to stay neutral as negating something that feels important but is perhaps hard to articulate? I would like to suggest that paying attention to their experiences of shame is one way in which consultants can take these responsibilities seriously.

Part 2: Shame as an opportunity to inquire

Conceptualising shame

Both contemporary scholarship and popular commentary tend to treat shame in quite an individualised way, generally characterising it as a sense of not living up to some kind of behavioural or moral standard. Perhaps, as a result, while it may be regarded as an important aspect of how children develop the ability to self-regulate (e.g. Tomkins in Sedgwick and Frank 1995), a propensity to shame is treated in therapy literature (e.g. Morrison 2011), education literature (e.g. Cozolino 2013) and in popular psychology or management theory (e.g. Brown 2007) as something people need to work through or overcome.

One could see this focus on individuals as the legacy of the Enlightenment's idealisation of human freedom or, more currently, as a manifestation of the contemporary neo-liberalist ideal that denies human interdependence and places the responsibility for success or failure in whichever context squarely with individuals (Brinkmann 2017). The negative associations of shame, however, go back to the story of Adam and Eve in *Genesis*, and, as Elias argues in *The Civilising Process* (1939), the evolution of shame and its gradual passing into the shadows of discourse can be seen as a key aspect of the move from pre-modern to modern Western societies. Considering topics as varied as sex education, blowing one's nose, marriage and the use of forks, Elias describes how the process of *civilisation* can be thought of as the replacement of violence as the primary means of regulating social conduct, with shame, culminating in experiencing shame itself being shameful. So, one can well imagine that the undesirability of shame is deeply socialised and why the desire for its avoidance or overcoming might seem self-evident. I believe this position becomes very ambiguous, however, if we consider shame as part of the moral processes involved in interdependence.

The contemporary American philosopher Krista Thomason characterises shame as a complex emotion that relates to 'the experience of tension between one's identity and one's self-conception' (Thomason 2018: 18). In Mead's terms, we might take identity here to mean what we find ourselves doing and 'self-conception' being how we judge what we do as from the internalised perspective of the communities whose membership is important to us. Rather than seeing shame as inherently undesirable or something to overcome, however, Thomason ascribes it moral value. She asserts that a propensity for shame demonstrates a willingness to give material weight to the perspectives of others; put another way, to feel shame is to show that we are open to moral criticism and recognise the standing of others as moral agents. This figures the feeling of shame as a necessary counterpart to having respect for others, and this is a form of taking our responsibility towards others seriously.

Now, if moral judgement includes taking into account one's own interests as described above and bodies interact with themselves as they interact with other bodies, then having respect for others goes hand in hand with self-respect. This means that shame and self-respect are counterparts in the same way that shame and respect for others are. However, unlike the intuitive relationship between seeing shame as response to a feeling of having negated the moral agency of others, shame and self-respect are more complexly related. I suggest that they can be regarded as having the same paradoxical relationship as our sense of freedom and constraint described earlier: our awareness of our previous experiences of shame as spontaneous responses influences our sense of social constraint, which then influences what we might feel shame about in the future and so on. This way of thinking about shame and self-respect as paradoxically related is important because it highlights how the triggers of shame responses might be difficult to identify: if they are responses to ourselves, then they could be under-acknowledged. In that case, experiences of shame may be useful starting points for reflexive inquiry into practice.

From a different perspective, the contemporary Australian gender and cultural theorist Elspeth Probyn (2005) draws on the work of the

20th-century Canadian psychologist and pioneer of affect theory Silvan Tomkins to describe shame as an affectual and psychological phenomenon that relates to *belonging*. For Probyn, shame is an ambivalent state that arises when the possibility of connection with others who are important to us is confronted with the possibility of humiliation and exclusion. This highlights how, first, shame arises when the aspects of membership that we value most are at risk, which accounts for different people feeling shame about different things; second, shame arises not at the moment of exclusion, but before this – when the possibility of connection still exists. Then, if shame may arise in relation to actual others or in relation to ourselves, then the threat of exclusion must encompass both communities of actual others with whom we engage directly *and* communities of others with whom we ideologically identify but may never have even met. Of course, real and ideological communities in these senses may coincide, both relying to varying degrees on extrapolations from experiences of encountering others. The distinction could therefore be regarded as simply drawing attention to the differing degree of immediacy of those experiences rather than trying to say anything more concrete.

Taking these perspectives together gives us a novel account of shame as *an emergent affectual response to conscious or unconscious experiences of tension between how we would like to see ourselves and how we might actually be being seen by others (and ourselves) in relation to aspects of our conduct that afford us membership of real and ideological communities that are important to us*. In the pragmatist conception of ethics, taking in the widest range of interests on the matter at hand and making a judgement based on all of them then necessarily involves respect and self-respect and therefore shame.

Reflexive inquiries into experiences of shame

Recalling that social objects according to Mead are the shared expectations about social conduct relating to particular social acts, the disruption of social objects that consultants bring about might well lead to people's sense of belonging being called into question. One way of thinking about what organisational consultants do is that they aim to provoke the evolution of social objects in more or less radical ways, or towards particular ends, which clients aren't able to do themselves. The disruption of established patterns of interaction may however lead to anxiety and resistance as the fragility of the social order is brought into view. As the instigators of such disruptions, consultants may well find themselves being identified with their clients' anxieties. This may lead to consultants finding themselves regularly at risk of feeling the anticipation of exclusion and hence experiencing shame when their memberships of communities that are important to them are called in to question.

While a habitual response to an emerging sense of shame might be to re-establish a sense of belonging that avoids the discomfort that the anticipation of exclusion brings about by, for example, reaffirming the norm that has been contravened, I suggest that staying with experiences of shame may offer fruitful openings for inquiry. Following my problematisation of the idea of neutrality in the first half of this chapter and the examples of consultants facing various quandaries, I would like to suggest that this needn't be just to do with the organisations that are being consulted to. Rather, it may be both in relation to the groups consultants are working with insofar as their experiences may arise from what is happening with their clients, and reflexively in relation to those of their own interests that may be being called out by the situation at hand.

I have found engaging with my own discomfort in the moments when I experience shame to lower my anxiety and provide a greater ability to rationally weigh the competing threats of exclusion and come to a view about what to do. In Mead's terms, I see this as a way to increase my potential for ethical judgement. Over time, this process of inquiry has settled into a heuristic of three questions that draw on the tentative distinction between real and ideological communities introduced above:

(A) What real communities do I feel at risk of being actually excluded from?
What norms might be being contravened giving rise to this experience and how might that help me understand what is important to the group I'm working with?

(B) Which ideological communities do I feel at risk of feeling excluded from?
What that affords me membership of those communities feels at stake and why is that important?

(C) How does this understanding inform what I do next?

Worked example

To illustrate how these questions can be used, and appreciating that (C) is difficult to assess in retrospect, I use questions (A) and (B) to explore the experience I recounted above of the team away day when my invitation to offer topics for the OST session was greeted with silence and I was awash with feelings that left me feeling nearly paralysed (Table 1.1).

Table 1.1 Three question heuristic: illustration

Questions	Illustrative analysis
(A) What real communities do I feel at risk of being actually excluded from? What norms might be being contravened giving rise to this experience and how might that help me understand what is important to the group I'm working with?	Primarily, the real community was the group of managers I was working with. I had worked with them before and wanted to continue to do so both because I enjoyed it and because it may lead to further work with them. One analysis is that my asking the group members to be open about how they would maintain the quality of their work through the restructure may have been heard as an invitation to engage with the possibility of losing their jobs and likely competition for positions between themselves. This might contravene the ostensible public service norm of selflessness, indicating that maintaining a sense of selfless public service is important in what group members do. This would make sense in the context of the difficult decisions they often need to take to support organisations in regulatory failure. Perhaps their responses to me might mirror the responses their interventions receive in their work. The public sector in the UK is also heavily performance-managed which might make the expectation of being judged to have underperformed habitual for me and others.
(B) Which ideological communities do I feel at risk of feeling excluded from? What that affords me membership of those communities feels at stake and why is that important?	Primarily the community of organisational consultants who use large group methods, which I wanted to continue to be a part of as at that time I saw this as a potential career. • Being regarded as competent in using these methods well; • Being regarded as able to deal with difficult situations; • Being regarded as helpful. These are important because I am committed to trying to do right by others; at the time, I was also hoping to be able to earn a living from this kind of work which relied on having a good reputation.

The analyses provided above are necessarily partial, but they do help to articulate some of the issues that were in play. Question (B) in particular points to how considerations about my own abilities were important to me but difficult to engage with. On reflection, they likely accounted for much more of what was going on in my feelings of paralysis than I was prepared to see at the time. Acknowledging that these considerations may be playing into my practice has helped me keep more in mind as I work with groups.

Final remarks

Given what I have said about the unpredictability of social life, it would be inconsistent to suggest that striving for neutrality isn't sometimes helpful and that inquiring in to experiences of shame may sometimes lead nowhere interesting. My claim in this chapter is rather more modest: based on a pragmatist understanding of experience, acknowledging that neutrality is an aspiration that may sometimes negate the moral importance of the consultant in material ways can offer a richer account of what is involved in the practice of organisational consulting.

This acknowledgement brings the competition of goods involved in ethical judgement more firmly into view and places new responsibilities on consultants who can no longer claim to be able to focus solely on their clients' needs. Further, if shame deters consultants from exploring aspects of experience that may be important in their work, then avoiding shame may limit consultants' potential for ethical judgement when ethics are construed in pragmatist terms. Inquiring reflexively into experiences of shame, by contrast, is one way in which we may increase our potential for ethical judgement and find new opportunities for action, which may provide a different basis for judging how to balance consultants' and clients' competing needs in everyday consulting interactions. If we value choice and freedom, then this seems to be something worth engaging with.

Notes

1 This chapter presents work that was first explored in the author's 2019 doctoral thesis entitled 'Researching Breakdowns Involving Shame: Reflexive Inquiry and the Practice of Ethical Organisation Development in a UK Government Agency' available at https://doi.org/10.18745/th.22555.

References

Bion, W.R. (1967) Notes on memory and desire. *The Psychoanalytic Forum* 2: 272–280.

Brinkmann, S. (2017) *Stand firm: Resisting the self-improvement craze.* Cambridge: Polity Press

Brown, B. (2007) *I thought it was just me (but it isn't).* New York: Penguin

Bushe, G. and Marshak, R. (2015) *Dialogic organization development.* Oakland, CA: Berrett-Koehler.

Cheung-Judge, M. (2012) The self as instrument: A cornerstone for the future of OD. *OD Practitioner* 44(2): 42–47.

Cheung-Judge, M. and Holbeche, L. (2015) *Organization development*, 2nd ed. London: Kogan Page.

Cozolino, L. (2013) *The social neuroscience of education.* New York: Norton.

Czander, W. and Eisold, K. (2003) Psychoanalytic perspectives on organizational consulting: Transference and counter-transference. *Human Relations* 56(4): 475–490.

Denzin, N.K. and Lincoln, Y.S. (2017) *The SAGE handbook of qualitative research*, 5th ed. London: SAGE.

Elias, N. (1939) *The civilizing process*, revised ed. [2000]. Oxford: Blackwell.

Gertler, B. and Izod, K. (2004) Modernism and postmodernism in group relations: A confusion of tongues. In S. Cytrynbaum and D.A. Noumair (eds.), *Group dynamics, organizational irrationality, and social complexity: Group relations reader 3.* Jupiter, FL: A.K. Rice Institute, 81–98.

Joas, H. (1997) *G.H. Mead: A contemporary re-examination of his thought.* Cambridge, MA: MIT Press.

Kilkauer, T. (2013) What is managerialism? *Critical Sociology* 41(7–8): 1103–1119.

Mead, G.H. (1923) Scientific method and the moral sciences. *International Journal of Ethics* 33: 229–247.

Mead, G.H. (1925) The genesis of the self and social control. *International Journal of Ethics* 35: 251–277.

Mead, G.H. (1934) *Mind, self, and society; from the standpoint of a social behaviourist,* 17th ed. [2015]. Chicago, IL: University of Chicago Press.

Mead, G.H. (1938) *The philosophy of the act.* Chicago, IL: University of Chicago Press.

Morrison, A.P. (2011) The psychodynamics of shame. In R.L. Dearing and J.P Tangney (eds.), *Shame in the therapy hour.* Washington, DC: American Psychological Association, 23–44.

Owen, H. (1992) *Open space technology: A user's guide.* Potomac, MD: Abbott Publishing.

Probyn, E. (2005) *Blush: Faces of shame.* Minneapolis: University of Minnesota Press.

Rainey Tolbert, M.A. and Hanafin, J. (2006) Use of self in OD consulting: What matters is presence. In B.B. Jones and M. Brazzel (eds.), *The NTL handbook of organization development and change: Principles, practices, and perspectives.* San Francisco, CA: Pfeiffer, 69–82.

Sedgwick, E.K. and Frank, A. (1995) *Shame and its sisters: A Silvan Tomkins reader.* Durham, NC: Duke University Press.

Schein, E.H. (1987) *Process Consultation: Its role in organization development.* Reading, MA: Addison Wesley Publishing Co.

Schein, E.H. (2011) *Helping: How to offer, give, and receive help.* San Francisco, CA: Berrett-Koehler.

Seashore, C.N., Shawer, M.N., Thompson, G. and Mattare, M. (2004) Doing good by knowing who you are: The instrumental self as an agent of change. *OD Practitioner* 36(3), 42–46.

Stacey, R. (2012) *Tools and techniques of leadership and management.* London: Routledge.

Thomason, K. (2018) *Naked: The dark side of shame.* New York: Oxford University Press.

Wolstein, B. (1988) *Essential papers on countertransference.* New York: New York University Press.

2

CONSULTING

FACILITATION AND SHAME: WORKING TOGETHER TO AVOID CHALLENGES TO OUR SENSE OF SELF IN THE RECOGNITION OF OTHERS

Graham Curtis

Introduction

As a consultant, I'm often asked to facilitate discussions between groups or teams to explore how they work together. My general experience is that the managers I work with take the nature of the work of a facilitator for granted; they assume the need for someone outside of their team to come and help them think together. In my discussions with other consultants and facilitators, I have come to understand that this assumption is a common one. I have become curious as to whether there is some unspoken purpose that is being fulfilled by the presence and practice of a facilitator that has emerged over time without anyone noticing it. In this chapter, using my reflections on interactions I had leading up to and including an away-day with a team of directors, I wanted to find out if there were generalisable observations that could be made about what is going on as we go about our work as consultant facilitators.

What is facilitation?

Heron (1977, 1989), Reason and Rowan (1981) and Reason (1988) argue that the role of facilitator emerged from the role of the therapist as described by Carl Rogers and person-centred therapy. In his work on client-centred therapy, Rogers uses examples of group therapy to suggest that groups grow a "remarkable cohesiveness that parallels the unity evident in individual therapy" (1951, p288). Rogers argues that there is the potential for a group by sharing their feelings, to transcend their own sense of self to become part of a supra-individual. He suggests that early hurtful experiences limit our ability as individuals to be closer to others, and through engaging with a group, people can experience themselves differently and redefine themselves in relation to others. The role of the facilitator is analogous to that of the therapist in working with groups to achieve such transcendence.

Harvey et al. (2002) suggest that the role of the facilitator can be defined as someone who engages with individuals and groups to enable them to understand the processes they have to go through to change aspects of their behaviour or attitudes to themselves, their work or others. They conclude that a facilitator is likely to need a set of core skills, including communication and interpersonal skills. The work of Harvey et al. (2002) is indicative of much of the literature on facilitation, in which authors hold the assumption that, when working with groups, an individual facilitator is making independent rational choices that lead towards a pre-planned outcome. This results in viewing the facilitator as separate from and acting upon a group. Bens (2005), Schwarz (2002), Hogan (2003), McCain and Tobey (2004), Unger et al. (2013), Bee and Bee (1998) and Mann (2007) are all examples of literature that describe facilitation in this way.

Alternatively, George Herbert Mead (1938) and his concept of the social object offers a different way of thinking about facilitation by analogy. He distinguishes between physical objects as things existing in nature, and therefore the objects of study by the natural sciences, and social objects that exist only in human experience and are therefore the proper objects of study in social science. Mead uses the example of markets to demonstrate what he means by social objects. When someone offers to buy food in a market, it involves a range of responses from those offering to sell food. In this interaction, those making the offer to buy food can only do so if they are able to know how to make that offer by taking the attitude of those who are selling the food, and likewise someone offering to sell food can only make that offer if they are able to take up the attitude, or the tendency to act, of the person offering to buy the food. People take up the social object through the experience of their unique histories, so the social object is never deterministic but arises through the idiosyncratic and historically derived experiences of those who are interacting to produce the expectations of a social object.

To translate this idea into understanding facilitation as a social object, the facilitator can only facilitate if he or she is able to take the attitude or the tendency to act of those who he or she is seeking to facilitate. Those being facilitated can only participate in being facilitated if they are able to take the attitude or the tendency to act of the facilitator. We can only do this through having experienced such events in the past and learned to play the game of participating in a facilitated group meeting. In my experience, in the social object of facilitation, we take for granted the existence of a pre-planned agenda usually set out by the facilitator. This agenda will often either tacitly or explicitly have pre-existing objectives or intended outcomes for the meeting. These facilitated meetings will often involve tools such as 360-degree feedback mechanisms and psychological instruments such as Myers Briggs Type Indicator (MBTI). According to Mead, the social object is particularised through our experience of specific situations such as the away-day with the directors I set out in the narrative below.

Mead's ideas enable a very different way of thinking about facilitation in comparison to other authors referenced above, which suggest a generalisable and decontextualised process. In their case, facilitation is a practice learned and applied by individuals, whereas facilitation viewed as a social object can be seen as a shared set of expectations that have emerged over time. These expectations then shape the social interaction in facilitated groups through ongoing gestures and responses through which participants constrain and enable each other. This helps us as consultant facilitators understand ourselves as participants in the processes of interaction that are continually emerging in a group, rather than as somehow being outside and acting upon it. From this perspective, I can then understand my sense of responsibility for the outcome of the away-day as having also emerged over time in response to the expectations I have of myself as a facilitator and that others, with whom I work, may also have of me.

A narrative account of the planning and implementation of a facilitated away-day with a group of directors

I was invited by Barbara, the chief executive of a charity to discuss with her the possibility of facilitating an away-day with her team of directors. I hadn't worked with the group before and I very much wanted to do so, not just to be able to work with a new group of senior managers, but because I also felt that a certain amount of kudos came with working with the chief executive officer (CEO) and directors. I was both excited and nervous about the work.

In several meetings leading up to the away-day, Barbara and I discussed and shaped the agenda. She was keen to develop a deeper sense of trust in her team. She said that she had previously used a psychological assessment tool called MBTI step II and was keen to use it again with the team to explore how their preferences and behaviours might be supporting or hindering their ability to work well together. I expressed some doubts about the tool and that I wasn't trained to use (the use of the tool is licensed by a company named OPP and one must be trained by them before they will allow its use). MBTI step II is built on another tool, MBTI step I. My experience of being trained in MBTI step I had been difficult.

In that training, I participated with others in learning about the tool and how to use it. The training was delivered in a way that instructed me in the purpose of the tool, how it was to be used in detail and which questions might best elicit understanding for the individuals undergoing the assessment. The process begins with a self-assessment, where the individual assesses themselves against a set of expected behaviours within each of the four dichotomies, which comprise an individual's personality type. They then see the results of a self-completed questionnaire, which also gives an assessment of their type. Through a discussion of the self-assessed type and the questionnaire assessment, an individual comes to understand their 'best-fit' type. During the training, I occasionally digressed in conversation with the person who was being assessed, and when I did this, I was instructed not to do so as it could result in my not passing the course. At the end of the training programme, I was watched by the trainers delivering the programme who were checking how well I had adhered to the prescribed process through performing a mock assessment with someone who was also undergoing the training. I found the training to be restrictive and formulaic and the experience of it to be frustrating and annoying. I was loath to engage with the training and the MBTI tool again. Nevertheless, Barbara insisted that she wanted to use it, so I agreed to undertake the training before the away-day to allow me to do so.

In a later meeting with Barbara, we further discussed the away-day and started to discuss how her interactions with directors were interpreted and resulted in changes to how they made decisions as a group. Barbara said that she often felt that the conversations between directors resulted in a defensive pattern where directors would defend themselves from each other, which she felt disabled the group in having productive conversations. I said that it seemed to me like a tennis match, whereby the issue would be knocked between the directors like a tennis ball in order to win points. I suggested that I bring a tennis ball with me to the away-day to illustrate the dynamic. She suggested an inflatable globe as an alternative (the organisation was an international development charity). We settled on a brief agenda for the day, which I wrote up and sent to her. I scoured the local shops for an inflatable globe without success. I eventually bought some balloons that I hoped would suffice.

As part of the agenda, we agreed to show a video of a TED talk given by Brene Brown on her research into shame that Barbara had seen and felt might be thought-provoking for the other participants. During our planning of the away-day, Barbara had discussed how important it was for the directors to feel able to be vulnerable enough with each other to share how they were feeling openly. We eventually settled on the following agenda for the day:

08.45	Tea and coffee
09.15	Reflection (Darren, fundraising director)
09.30	360 Feedback
	What sense can we make of the 360 feedback? What are our strengths and weaknesses individually and as a team? How will we respond to them?
11.00	Break for coffee
11.15	MBTI Step II: Understanding our impact on each other and the wider organisation in times of change
	We will share our reflections and learning from our Step II profile and how our preferences show up in our work. How do we enable and constrain each other, especially in our response to decision-making and change?
13.00	Lunch Discussions: Following up on SMG: Next Steps
14.00	How do we use our authority individually and collectively? Can we be different together?
15.30	Our Commitments for the Future

>   In order to become a digital and global organisation, what will we need to do to lead the organisation well?
>   What do we need to do differently now, individually and collectively, to give us the best possible chance of success in the future?
>   How will we hold each other accountable for the change?
> **17.00** Close

It is my experience that this type of agenda is a typical outcome of planning such away-days. It represents a series of planned sessions with predetermined outcomes that gives the participants some comfort about what to expect on the day. Barbara said that she planned to send it to the directors only a couple of days ahead of the away-day to avoid them becoming anxious about it. My assumption was that Barbara was imagining the directors having a sense of anxiety about what they might be expected to do together on the day and wanted to limit the time that they might experience such anxiety. She also made reference to feelings of vulnerability as she was feeling a little trepidatious ahead of the away-day. I replied with my thanks and that I too was also feeling a little anxious in my anticipation of it.

Facilitating the away-day

On the day of the away-day, I had arranged for the room to have six comfortable chairs organised in a circle without a table in the middle. As we entered the room and the directors saw how it had been arranged, Sharon, the director of policy, suggested we shouldn't make anything of her sitting near the door and Neil, the international director, suggested it was good not to have a table between us and Barbara made a joke about expecting something like a therapy session. Their comments came in rapid succession and there was a lot of nervous laughter at these exclamations. I was privately curious as to what these comments might be about. I welcomed everyone to the workshop and explained that we were going to start with a video from Brene Brown about her research into shame. I then started the video and we all watched it.

A video about shame

In the video (Brown, 2020) Brene Brown describes how, in her research, she came to the conclusion that vulnerability is essential to wholehearted living (in the video she does not describe what wholehearted living is and seems to expect the audience to take a mutual understanding of that for granted). She describes this through a narrative of a conversation with a friend which was confessional in nature and was in itself describing a form of confessional speech in a previous video appearance Brown had made. The public confession seems to be important for her in what she describes as a personal transformational experience. Foucault and Hurley (1998, p63) describe how in modern society the confession as a religious act has been employed in a series of relationships, including that of patient and therapist. If we take up the idea that the role of the facilitator has emerged from the role of the therapist (Heron 1977, 1989; Reason & Rowan 1981; Reason, 1988), then maybe the social object of facilitation as some sort of public or group confessional with me as facilitator/priest is what was going on here. It is maybe no wonder then that the group entered the room with some trepidation.

Brown (2020) goes on in the video to suggest that vulnerability is the birthplace of innovation, creativity and change. She seems to locate shame as an individual experience expressed through internal conversation with what she calls a little gremlin. She argues that shame is destructive and highly correlated with addiction, depression, violence and aggression.

The video ended and there was a moment of quiet in the room. I started the conversation by bringing attention to the comments people had made on the way into the room and wondered aloud what they might have indicated, as I did so I felt that I was drawing attention to something that may be important as an indicator of how this group expected to work together and how comfortable they might be as a group in talking about their feelings. I asked whether their comments had come from a sense of anxiety that the room had been arranged differently to how they usually met. Sharon said that she had been joking and there seemed to be some awkwardness between all of us. There followed a long pause, there seemed to be no one who wanted to pick up the questions about what their comments on entering the room might mean.

Using 360 Feedback and Competency Frameworks

I moved on to briefly explain the agenda that Barbara and I had prepared and suggested we move onto the first session on the agenda. The directors had all received individual reports, called 360 feedback reports, in recent weeks. These reports were compiled from submissions from people who were managed by the directors, some of whom were peers, and there was also a response from Barbara as their manager. The feedback was in response to questions as to how well the directors were demonstrating the behaviours that are described in the organisation's competency framework. In arranging the workshop, Barbara and I had agreed to show the individual director scores and an average against each competency anonymously. This meant that only the individual directors knew which scores were theirs, but they could see how their score matched up against other directors' scores.

I asked the directors what sense they were making of it. Neil said that having the data displayed competitively in the way it was may not be helpful, like a football league table. Neil's comment made me feel a little defensive and I responded by suggesting that the data had been set out in a comparative format and that didn't necessarily mean that it was competitive. As we made our way through each competency, Sharon said that she didn't want to appear difficult, but without knowing from whom the feedback was coming she found it hard to understand the context of the comments and scores.

As I reflect on this interaction, I am struck by Neil's comments about feeling that the data was creating competition between the directors. I presumed that he meant that he was having his behaviour compared to that of others in a way that those who demonstrated the behaviours set out in the competency framework best would be looked on more favourably than those who did not. I notice that I discounted this and instead made a gesture to suggest that they were in fact comparative rather than competitive. On reflection, there seems little difference between competitive and comparative, given that the standard of expected behaviour was being dictated by a set of generalised, desired behaviours within a competency framework that does not pay any attention to the context and relationships that prompted the feedback. I am also struck by the comment from Sharon. I can see that she was reflexively pointing out the challenge of using such tools out of context whilst anticipating that her remarks might be taken as being resistant. Sharon's comments about context were never taken up, and yet it seems they are important reflexive questions about the validity of the competency framework. I am left wondering what would have happened if we had been able to have a conversation that could have legitimately challenged the usefulness of it as a tool in their particular context. It seemed to me that what happened was very little, in that although we discussed the feedback, it was in a fairly cursory way that did little to enlighten or help with any understanding of the way that this group worked together.

Three-hundred-and-sixty-degree feedback processes and competency frameworks take for granted that the skills and competencies in any given situation are located in individuals and the purpose of the feedback is to show how managers are doing in demonstrating their level of competency against any given indicator. The job of the individual is, therefore, to consider this feedback and change their behaviour accordingly to better demonstrate what is required. Cognitivist psychology and strategic choice theory (Stacey, 2007) underpin competency frameworks and 360-degree feedback. In these processes, feedback loops are used to measure performance against expectation and highlight adjustments to be made to the human systems (in this case, the directors) to improve performance. The relevance and generalisability of the competency framework is taken for granted and unchallenged. Challenges to the relevance of any given competency framework would be likely to be interpreted as resistance and would require further training. Stacey (2012) refers to competency frameworks as techniques of instrumental rationality and argues that they are instruments of disciplinary power to which everyone is then subjected, even those leaders who design them. In considering my own experience of working in organisations and using competency frameworks, I would agree with Stacey that they are often used in a disciplinary way to constrain and encourage particular behaviours. Perhaps it was this sense of being disciplined and constrained that Sharon and Neil were responding to.

Using the Myers Briggs Type Indicator

We stopped for a coffee, and when we returned, we moved on to look at what the MBTI assessments could show us about how they were likely to respond to each other and as a group.

I asked the directors to place their Post-it Notes on the areas that related to their reported profile. As they moved around the room deciding where to place their Post-it Notes, I found myself directing people to move on, chivvying them along much as a teacher would do to errant pupils. As I noticed that I was doing this, I caught myself acting in a way that I hadn't intended but that I felt was both appropriate and inappropriate at the same time. It seemed to me that no one was paying any attention to me behaving in this way other than to do as I asked, nor did anyone object.

The MBTI tool was derived from the work of Carl Jung by Katharine Cook Briggs and Isabel Briggs Myers. The company who own the copyright to the tool and who also provide the training to use it claim that is based on the typological theories proposed by Carl Jung in his book *Psychological Types* (Sharp, 1987). The tool consists of a questionnaire and an assessment process which seeks to uncover innate preferences. There is a parallel here with the use of the 360 feedback as a tool in the preceding session. Both tools take for granted an individual psychology within which individuals can learn about their own mental models through external feedback processes and, in uncovering this, can make individual choices to change the way they behave to better align with what is expected of them.

I notice how, in examining people's behaviours using the MBTI tool, the motivation and responsibility for how the directors behave is rooted in them as individuals and their innate typology, therefore the dynamics of the group can only be understood through how each of these individual types interact with each other to create an outcome. I also note how this process places me in the position of knowledge and authority as the sole arbiter of the process and the only one qualified to use the tool. It may not be so surprising then that I was tempted into taking the position of the teacher with the directors as my pupils in a dynamic with me as the expert and them as compliant novices.

Trying to notice how we were relating together using a balloon

In the afternoon of the away-day, we started with a session entitled: How do we use our authority individually and collectively? Can we be different together? In this session, I tried to allow the process of relating to emerge from the interactions in the group. I was keen to move away from a prescribed process towards a more open conversation. Barbara explained that she had been approached by a member of the policy team directly who had expressed concern about a piece of work that had been done by the communications team which used dogs' behaviour to illustrate issues of gender.

The member of the policy team had felt that the work would be perceived as frivolous and inappropriate. Barbara had suggested that the work not be published in any way until there had been a wider discussion as to whether and how it would be used. This was somehow translated by others in the organisation into a message that Barbara had not liked the work and had it stopped. As the directors discussed the issue, other examples were introduced to illustrate similar patterns. Sharon suggested it might be better for them to share their plans at the earliest opportunity to enable a more thorough discussion as they progressed. She used an example of how the decision by the finance directorate to set carbon budgets had not been fully discussed and had resulted in overly tight budgets that didn't allow the appropriate level of travel. Terry, the finance director, responded that his department had been given the task of setting the carbon budgets and they had apportioned them according to headcount. There followed a fairly tense exchange between Sharon and Terry about whether carbon budgets were useful or not, which seemed to demonstrate the pattern of defensiveness that Barbara and I had discussed in our planning conversations.

I took this as a prompt for me to interrupt the flow of the discussion by blowing up a balloon. I introduced the idea that to avoid the conversation ending up in a defensive argumentative pattern, perhaps we could use the balloon to refocus the issue into the centre of the room. I suggested that this might help them to notice the patterns that were emerging between them, thus introducing the process that I had agreed with Barbara in our planning of the day. This shift, from allowing the conversation to emerge organically to directing it using the balloon, resulted in a passing of the balloon when people started talking, with it moving between individuals and the centre of the room. I suggested that we return to the example of the carbon budgets and how it might have been improved by them each sharing their plans earlier to enable better agreement on such issues. Neil responded that he would find it difficult to do so. He used militaristic metaphors to suggest that he needed to defend his teams. I noticed the militaristic language and asked Neil what the use of those kinds of metaphors might mean for him. He appeared to stop short, he said he didn't know, and that he would need to think about it further. I suggested that others in the room may feel similarly and thanked him for being willing to respond in the way that he had. I asked for views from the rest of the directors, but no one seemed willing to continue to explore it. Sharon started to talk about what she called the 'myth' of how Barbara's decisions about what she did and didn't like was patterned across the organisation. I suggested that the word 'myth' might be important and that they might explore it, I was hoping that the group would use my invitation to explore the power dynamics between them. However, my invitation wasn't picked up by anyone in the room and the conversation continued as if I had not said anything. The session ended with us breaking for coffee and with a recognition of this myth-building being important but without a resolution about how they might want to try to change it together.

In this session, I was attempting to use the balloon to offer a new way for the group to discuss their relationships. However, on reflection, in doing so I was still focusing on the binary interaction of two individuals and missing the wider impact of the dynamics of the group. With the use of the balloon, I was exercising power over what happened within the group and deciding through my intervention what we should talk about and how we should talk about it. It's curious that the directors agreed to my working with them in this way. There was little to no resistance to my directive way of facilitating. It seems to me that in taking up the disciplining and constraining processes I have described earlier, I participated in a pattern of behaviour that I, and the rest of the group, had created together without being aware we were doing so. Neil, in his reaction to the request from Barbara for the directors to share their plans at an earlier stage, indirectly expressed how vulnerable this made him feel and that he felt unable to do it. The reaction from the group was to become quiet. People seemed unsure what to do next; it seemed to me that at this point, there was potential for something different to happen. In my asking Neil what might be significant about his use of militaristic language, I was seeking to explore how Neil had expressed himself and whether this may have been something shared in the group. However, in a similar way to my offering a discussion about their initial comments as they entered the room, the idea wasn't taken up and, after a pause, the discussion fell into what seemed a pattern where they acted in a way that was familiar and usual. It seems that when moments offering the potential for novelty arose in our relating together there followed a pause, as if no one knew what to do in facing a moment that had not been encountered before and which did not follow a familiar pattern. In these moments it felt to me as if time was suspended until I or someone else was able to say something that re-engaged us back into a known pattern of relating that allowed us to continue. It led me to wonder whether a pattern of relating had emerged that helped maintain the status quo in response to the anticipation of feelings of shame that are caused by an unpredictable future. This echoes Brene Brown's (2020) suggestion that vulnerability and therefore the risk of shame are core to novelty and innovation.

A Disappointing End to the Day

I remember being disappointed by the discussion in the group in the last session. The conversation became rather mundane as the group made plans for some minor changes to the way they worked together and how they communicated with others in the organisation. I felt that very little had shifted in how the group worked together as a result of the day we had spent together. As I write, I still feel that I participated in a set piece of relatively predictable conversations in which we all, as participants, contrived to stay within a pattern of relating to which we all had become accustomed and which felt safe. I became curious as to what the purpose might be of planning the processes involved in the away-day to provide a safe yet apparently constraining environment.

Feeling shame at the idea of infantilising others

As part of my doctoral work on organisational process, I shared this narrative along with some early ideas as to what I might focus on in my research with the learning set I was working with. During a discussion about the narrative above, one of my learning set colleagues suggested that the use of toys such as balloons in team meetings can be infantilising for the participants. I was shocked, but even as I mentally started to defend my actions to myself, I recognised some truth in the idea. I certainly hadn't intended to infantilise anyone and I felt shame at the idea that I might have done so, but I couldn't deny it as a reasonable explanation for the compliant responses from the participants at the away-day. I think the combination of feelings of shame and experiencing learning at the same time, prompted some movement in my thinking about what was going on in my practice as a facilitator.

What is shame?

While discussing this project with my learning set, we talked about the difference between shame and guilt. The general point of view was that shame was an individually felt affect resulting from feeling socially exposed as inferior, whereas guilt arises as a result of having done something that is seen by yourself and potentially others as wrong. I took from that conversation that shame is about how we are seen by others and, in turn, how we view ourselves. The conversation resulted in a definite sense that feelings of shame required us to be publicly exposed in some way. However, this way of describing shame did not resonate with me. My recollection of having experienced feelings of shame did not necessarily involve being publicly exposed. Dearing and Tangney (2002, p15) state that in empirical studies, there is little difference between people reporting solitary shame experiences. In studies, 17.2% of children reported experiencing solitary shame. Similarly, in adults, 16.5% reported experiencing solitary shame experiences. So, it seems that in studies people have reported feelings of shame without being publicly exposed. Dearing and Tangney (ibid, p17) go on to suggest that there is little difference in what sort of event or behaviour might induce shame, stating that in their study, respondents gave similar examples. They argue that shame is an individually felt affect, that is, about who we perceive ourselves to be in response to others. Shame seems to cause us to need to be not who we are, resulting in a wish to run away, or to hide or to avoid the situation.

If solitary shame is possible, then what might be going on in processes of shame if it is not necessarily about being publicly exposed? Stacey (2007), Stacey et al. (2000), Griffin (2002) and Mowles (2015) draw on the thinking of George Herbert Mead, Norbert Elias and John Dewey, among others, to propose that the individual and the social are the singular and the plural of an ongoing process. Mead (1934, p178) proposes that the self-consciousness of individuals emerges from the private conversations in which one becomes an object to oneself. This involves a 'Me' (an identity), which is the generalised attitude of a group taken towards oneself. The individual's response to this me is the 'I', which is the spontaneous response to the individual's perception of the group's view of him/herself. This 'I' response is potentially novel and therefore offers the possibility of change in one's sense of identity. Individually, the 'I' and the 'Me' represent a paradoxical phenomenon in which the 'I' can only be understood in response to the 'Me'. It is important to understand that Mead describes the 'I' and the 'Me' as inseparable elements of an ongoing process.

If we take up Mead's (ibid) suggestion that our sense of identity emerges as a result of the I/Me dialectic, then who we are must be fundamentally social. If we are faced with a situation where the assumed attitude of others in our social situation causes our 'I' to cast doubt on our previous understanding of our 'Me' regardless of whether that doubt is publicly known, a feeling of shame can result, as we can no longer be who we thought we were. This gives us an explanation of how feelings of solitary shame can be experienced as a private and individual experience but is nevertheless part of a social process.

Processes of learning involving shame

Aram (2001) suggests that shame experiences are inevitably induced in a learning process. She suggests that a learning process (she uses the examples of university learning or therapy) involves accepting that there is something which we do not know which, in turn, results in a loss of the power of knowing and a challenge to our sense of who we are, thus giving rise to feelings of shame. I think Aram is describing significant learning processes that offer the risk of a change in our sense of self. Learning processes that are potentially transformational of our identity. If the away-day is an intended learning process that is potentially transformative of those involved and the way they work together, then, according to Aram, processes of shame, which she suggests may come in the guise of anger, contempt or withdrawal, will be inevitable. Aram describes the paradoxical way in which the destructiveness of shame is at the same time potentially, but not necessarily, creative. This point is missed by Brene Brown (2020), who seems to see shame as an entirely negative phenomenon. Aram (2001) describes this feeling of shame as being the individually felt instances of incremental transformations of identity that occur in groups as people make meaning together as an emergent property of their interaction. Thinking now about the away-day, I think we missed an opportunity to work reflexively with the dynamics of the group and the feelings of shame that such work might have created. I think, instead, we worked together as a group in a planned way to maintain familiar patterns of relating to avoid or minimise the discomfort of shame.

Elias describes a civilising process of human society based on an increasing sense of shame:

> The feeling of shame is a specific excitation, a kind of anxiety which is automatically reproduced in the individual on certain occasions by force of habit. Considered superficially it is fear of degradation or, more generally, of other people's gestures of superiority.
>
> (2000, p415)

Elias proposes that people are susceptible to other people's gestures of superiority if they accord with the:

> agency of self-constraint implanted in the individual by others on whom he was dependent, who possessed superiority over him ... The conflict expressed in shame-fear is not merely a conflict of the individual with the prevalent society of opinion; the individual's behaviour has brought him into conflict with part of himself that represents this social opinion.
>
> (ibid, p415)

The work of Elias is resonant with that of Mead in recognising identity emerging from social processes. It is the bringing together of the thinking of Mead's and Elias's perspectives that Aram (2001) uses when she describes shame as being inevitable in situations where there is potential for transformation. Mowles (2015) draws on the thinking of Hegel as he describes this dialectical process of movement between polarities of paradox, such as the individual forming and being formed by the social at the same time as being inherent in our experience of participating in groups. The thinking of Mead, Elias and Mowles helps me to understand shame as an individually felt effect of a social process. It is this taking on of the attitude of others that allows our sense of self to continuously emerge in a private I/Me dialogue that results in a sense of shame as our identity shifts, as we respond to the gestures of others in our social interactions.

Concluding thoughts: working together to avoid the risk of shame

It is easy to understand that we might want to avoid putting ourselves at risk of experiencing the discomfort of shame. If we are to do so, we would have to work together through our gestures and responses in the groups in which we work to maintain familiar patterns of relating to avoid the potential for novelty. I can understand how anyone attempting to introduce novel ways of relating could easily find themselves being ignored or even resisted.

If we take up this way of thinking about individuals and groups, then our participation inevitably has the potential to provoke feelings of shame. If it is our intention to explore and change how we relate to each other in groups, then it is important that we attempt to deal reflexively with and be prepared to discuss feelings as they arise in the social processes of us acting together. Or, as Stacey (2012, p89) puts it, "Thinking together about what we are doing and why we are doing it seems to me to be the only way to produce reasonable and lasting changes in what we do".

When I was confronted with the idea that my facilitation practice was infantilising, working in this reflexive way, staying with my own feelings of shame and struggling to understand and learn through the experience, has enabled me to continue my research into my practice and develop new ways of thinking about it.

In attempting to use these differing perspectives to understand what was going on in the away-day with these directors, it seems to me that the working assumptions of the group belong to the perspective on groups defined by a humanistic perspective. This is demonstrated by Barbara as the group leader in her desire for the away-day to enable the group, through a form of confessional process, to reach for alignment through which they can transcend the individual and attain a state where they represent the kind of supra-individual described by Rogers (1951, p288). It is possible that the nervous remarks of Sharon and Barbara at the beginning of the away-day were responding to that possibility. It is also interesting that the group's response to my attempts to discuss their remarks at the beginning of the day and my offer of picking up the mythical nature of the discussion resulted in a minimisation and dismissal of their importance, perhaps to avoid any new patterns of behaviour emerging and thereby negating the risk of any feelings of shame. Mead (1934, p179) describes how in the conversation of gesture and response an individual takes the attitude of the other towards his or her own stimulus. If we take up Mead's perspective and see shame as the individually felt effect of changing group dynamics and we take up the idea of an individual taking the attitude of the other in his own stimulus, then in a social situation where the potential for shame is present it must be shared by others in the group. It seems likely then that we were all complicit in maintaining the patterns of relating to which we had become accustomed, perhaps to avoid the potential for shame to arise in the ensuing challenges to our sense of identity and to maintain familiar patterns of relating.

The planning of the away-day was, in some way, an effort to reduce discomfort for the other participants and for ourselves, as evidenced by Barbara holding back the agenda for the day and yet at the same time wanting to have the potential for transformational learning to take place. In short, Barbara and I wanting to have our cake and eat it in trying to predict and manage the feelings of shame that might be provoked, and in doing so, attempting to instrumentalise that shame for a particular outcome. Furthermore, our deployment of anonymised tools such as 360 feedback mechanisms and decontextualised competency frameworks and tools such as MBTI may be offering the potential for understanding oneself in a formulaic and known way that minimises the potential for shame to be experienced by the group.

As I have said earlier in this chapter, within the community of people working on the Doctor of Management programme with whom I shared my work, some have pointed to the potential for the work with the balloon to lead to infantilisation of the group. It's clear that the use of a child's toy such as a balloon brings the potential for infantilisation into sharp focus. However, the processes of 360 feedback tools and psychometrics such as MBTI, through their unchallengeable foundations and generalisability as well as tight facilitator-led processes involving flip charts and posters and balloon, also seem to me to be designed to produce dependence upon the facilitator in such group meetings, perhaps as a defence against anxiety rather than the rational analytical tools they appear to be. Using planned agendas and these tools and techniques, the facilitator (in this case, me) in collusion with the leader (in this case, Barbara) can maintain a position of power in the group and co-create a dynamic of dependence from the group on the facilitator. The dependent dynamic of such facilitator-led meetings could be interpreted as infantilising in its very nature whilst purporting to be about encouraging participation and transformation. It would seem such infantilising practices are common with Mowles (2007, 2009) describing the use of pipe cleaners, Play-Doh, balloons and bits of cardboard as well as very strict facilitator-led rules in meetings intended to support people to come together to create organisational strategy. Crewe (2014) also points to the use of coloured stickers, Post-it Notes and flip chart paper in what she describes as rituals of visioning the future in international development organisations. I'm drawn to the moment of clarity and realisation I had in the midst of the MBTI part of the away-day when I experienced myself acting, unresisted by the group, as if I was a teacher directing errant pupils. For me, this moment clearly demonstrates the power dynamics of the group in service of maintaining the reiteration of familiar patterns of relating. When I made attempts at changing the pattern of the conversation through noticing the pattern (e.g. the use of mythical language) and inviting conversation about it, the group dismissed this by pausing and then ignoring it and carrying on with their previous conversation.

On reflection, I have come to think that the way the day was planned and the assumptions that Barbara and I were making in such planning were ultimately denying others the opportunity to participate in how the day would proceed. And yet, it seems that their expectation of Barbara providing an agenda for the day, their acceptance of the agenda and their compliant participation on the day would suggest that they wanted and expected such planning and forming of an agenda to take place. If the use of the balloon or perhaps even the away-day as a whole in its planning and the way it transpired on the day was in any way infantilising, maybe such infantilisation is an emergent property of the gestures and responses of me, Barbara and the rest of the group as we engaged in the social object of facilitation.

Mowles (2009), through his experience as a consultant facilitator, describes a similar dynamic to the one I have set out. He depicts a group resisting his attempts to change the expected dynamic of meeting together with a pre-prepared agenda with specific intended outcomes to a more exploratory and emergent way of working, even to the point of criticising his capability as a facilitator in suggesting that he wasn't in control of the workshop. Mowles argues that to reflect together on our actions in an authentic sense requires us to recognise each other, and in doing so, risks the inevitable change in our sense of self. As I have argued in this chapter, it is this reflecting on our acting together and the unknown impact on our own sense of self that causes the potential for the occurrence of feelings of shame. Mowles (ibid.) further argues that facilitation is a form of temporary leadership in which:

> The ethical and performative challenge for the consultant seems to me to reside in these junctures of negotiation, where we have a genuine

opportunity for the recognition of others and alternative understanding of what is possible. The difference that I think a consultant can bring is to exercise a temporary form of leadership by taking part in, and encouraging negotiation as a way of helping permanent members of staff to see each other anew.

(ibid., p291)

By reflecting on my practice as a facilitator, I think I have been able to better recognise myself in my own practice and my interdependence with those with whom I work. I have come to understand that it is easy to, perhaps even difficult not to, collude with groups in the avoidance of mutual recognition and the inevitably ensuing shame. As I have shared this thinking with others, they too have recognised what I have been describing in their own experience of facilitating.

I agree with Mowles (2009) that this is the ethical and performative challenge that we face as we practice as facilitators and consultants. As facilitators, rather than seeing ourselves as applying tools and techniques from outside of the groups we work with, it may be that we can offer an opportunity to support others to recognise the shared nature of uncomfortable emotions such as shame and get some comfort from that as we all struggle together with our ongoing dilemmas.

References

Aram, E. (2001) The Experience of Complexity: Learning as the Potential Transformation of Identity, unpublished thesis, University of Hertfordshire.

Bee, F. and Bee, R. (1998) *Facilitation Skills (Training Essentials)*, London: Chartered Institute of Personnel & Development.

Bens, I. (2005) *Advanced Facilitation Strategies: Tools and Techniques to Master Difficult Situations*, San Francisco, CA: Jossey-Bass.

Brown, B. (2020) Listening to Shame. Accessed at https://www.ted.com/talks/brene_brown_listening_to_shame?language=en on 14th September 2020.

Crewe, E. (2014) Doing Development Differently: Rituals of Hope and Despair in an INGO: *Development in Practice*, Vol 24, No 1, pp91–104.

Dearing, R. L. and Tangney, J. P. (2002) *Shame and Guilt*, New York: Guilford Publications.

Elias, N. (2000) *The Civilizing Process*, Oxford: Blackwell Publishing.

Foucault, M. and Hurley, R. (1998) *The History of Sexuality: The Will to Knowledge: V. 1: The Will to Knowledge*, London: Penguin Books.

Griffin, D. (2002) *The Emergence of Leadership, Linking Self Organisation and Ethics*, London: Routledge.

Harvey, G., Loftus-Hills, A., Titchen, A., Kitson, A., McCormack, B. and Seers, K. (2002) Getting Evidence into Practice: The Role and Function of Facilitation: *Journal of Advanced Nursing*, Vol 37, No 6, pp577–588.

Heron, J. (1977) *Dimensions of Facilitator Style*, London: Human Potential Research Project.

Heron, J. (1989) *The Facilitator's Handbook*, London: Kogan Page.

Hogan, C. (2003) *Practical Facilitation: A Toolkit of Techniques*, London: Kogan Page.

Mann, T. (2007) *Facilitation: An Art, Science, Skill or All Three? Build Your Expertise in Facilitation*, London: Resource Productions.

McCain, D. V. and Tobey, D. D. (2004) *Facilitation Basics (ASTD Training Basics)*, 2nd edn, Alexandria: ATD Press.

Mead, G. H. (1934) *Mind, Self, and Society: From the Standpoint of a Social Behaviourist*, Chicago, IL: University of Chicago.

Mead, G. H. (1938) *The Philosophy of the Act*, Chicago, IL: University of Chicago Press.

Mowles, C. (2007) Promises of Transformation: Just How Different are International Development NGOs? *Journal of International Development*, Vol 19, No 3, pp401–411.

Mowles, C. (2009) Consultancy as Temporary Leadership: Negotiating Power in Everyday Practice: *International Journal of Learning and Change*, Vol 3, No 3, pp281–293.

Mowles, C. (2015) *Managing in Uncertainty: Complexity and the Paradoxes of Everyday Organisational Life*, London: Routledge.

Reason, P. (1988). *Human Inquiry in Action: Developments in New Paradigm Research*, London: Sage.

Reason, P. and Rowan, J. (1981) *Human Inquiry: A Sourcebook of New Paradigm Research*, London: Wiley.

Rogers, C. R. (1951) *Client-Centred Therapy*, London: Constable and Robinson.

Schwarz, R. M. (2002) *The Skilled Facilitator: A Comprehensive Resource for Consultants, Facilitators, Managers, Trainers, and Coaches*, 3rd edn, San Francisco, CA: Jossey-Bass.

Sharp, D. (1987) *Personality Types, Jung's Model of Typology*, Toronto: Inner City Books.
Stacey, R. D., Griffin, D. and Shaw, P. (2000) *Complexity and Management: Fad or Radical Challenge to Systems Thinking*, London: Routledge.
Stacey, R. D. (2007) *Strategic Management and Organisational Dynamics*, 5th edn, London: Pearson Education.
Stacey, R. D. (2012) *Tools and Techniques of Leadership and Management*, London: Routledge.
Unger, R., Nunnally, B. and Willis, D. (2013) *Designing the Conversation: Techniques for Successful Facilitation*, Indianapolis, IN: New Riders Publishing.

3

WHAT ARE CONSULTANTS ACTUALLY RECOGNISED FOR?

Eric Wenzel[1]

Introduction

Throughout my career in consulting, I have revisited an experience that I think poses a practical challenge for most organisational consultants: the phenomenon of finding myself being (re)invited by clients and consultant colleagues to engage in organisational change in planned ways despite the shared experience that such projects rarely go according to the plans we devise (Honneth, 1994, 2001; Griffin, 2002; Shaw, 2002; Stacey, 2007, 2010). The conflict that I inevitably encounter when projects go astray has often led me to question my ability to lead these projects. However, if clients and colleagues (re)invite me to work with them, I must be contributing something, even if it is not what they explicitly expect of me. When I began to ponder what it is I am recognised for, it turned out that it was my ability to tolerate the unpredictability naturally arising from my work better than those I come to work for and with. In other words, it is paradoxically only in the opening up of the possibility for misrecognition that I am actually recognised.

As a consequence, my definition of success has shifted from actually reaching a predetermined goal to supporting clients in making better sense of their current practice whilst struggling on their way towards this or that goal. I find this particularly useful because it may lead to an enhanced comprehension of repeatedly enacted patterns of interaction and, importantly, a debate about their usefulness. Failure might then be described as an inability of the members of a group to reflect upon their generalised tendencies to act in ways that would heighten their awareness of how they contribute to the patterns of interaction they find themselves caught up in. In that sense, I have come to understand my main contribution to be constantly opening up and revisiting our assumptions about what we are actually doing against the backdrop of the programmes I am contracted to deliver while coping with the uncertainty of not knowing what is going to happen over the full course of these programmes. In this light, it seems to me I both support clients to redefine their organisational context and help them to come to terms with the redefinition of their self-perception in this context. The same holds for my co-operation with consultant colleagues; consulting firms appear to mirror the dynamics of their client organisations in that sense.

So while ostensibly my work has to do with conveying techniques for providing leadership or defining targets and methods for successful roll-outs, I have begun to take seriously my experience of receiving recognition for the ability to point out opportunities, however minimal they may be, to renegotiate reflexively and think about why we are doing what we are doing as we struggle to implement strategies, besides tolerating the potential for misrecognition for doing just that. To try and promote reflection on our joint efforts may invite misrecognition of me as consultant for several reasons. The most obvious one arises from the tension that emerges when I invite clients to think about why it is so appealing to talk about the often-idealised future outcomes my work is said to yield and what it is that we are avoiding talking about when we are trying to map out a future which cannot be foreseen, let alone planned.

I will begin by giving an account of a project for management and organisational development which a colleague of mine and I conducted for a client of ours. I will give examples of unplanned and conflictual instances with senior managers to elaborate my ideas on issues of human relations of recognition and power. I will outline the way we saw our own practice as based on ideas of dominant systemic thinking and I will use the "consulting cycle" (Cockman et al., 1999) and Edgar Schein's (1999/2009) advice for successful culture change as the theoretical basis of such thinking. This will meet a critical review of our approach by contrasting it with the theory of complex responsive processes of relating (Griffin, 2002; Stacey, 2007) and theories of recognition (Hegel, 1977; Honneth, 1994), which I will use to put forward a different understanding of how change in organisations comes about, one which is not so much concerned with planning, but which embraces ideas of conflict in order to make sense of my own experience differently.

A leadership development programme that meets with resistance

A while ago, I was involved in an organisational development initiative with a Japanese automobile supplier's (AAE) German organisation. We (a consultant colleague Gavin and I) were called to have a conversation with representatives of the board and the German vice president (VP) of human resources (HR) because the company had been facing a downturn in their business for over two years after 15 years of constant growth. The chief executive officer (who, like most of the board members and the VP of HR, was Japanese) was very clear in his assessment of what developments had led to the current state of affairs. In his view, most senior and middle managers did not live up to the clearly defined company values of "Creation," "Passion" and "Challenge." For him, those values were at the core of the organisation, and if the managers would take them to heart in their daily work, business would be impacted in the most positive way. When asked what those values actually meant and how one could determine whether a manager lived in accordance with them, the answer was rather unclear. Since the values were based on an essentially Japanese understanding of how to lead, there was a sense that only Japanese employees would ever be able to grasp their meaning in full.

Setting the programme up

We thought that what the CEO meant by his interpretation of values would be unclear to other managers, and so our proposal was to conduct interviews with representatives of different parts of the organisation, summarise the main points we learned throughout these interviews and compare and contrast them with the board's views. This last step would be the subject of a workshop with the board members and HR representatives. Our suggestion was supported by the board.

The German organisation was divided into three main departments (Original Equipment Manufacturer [OEM],[2] Aftermarket[3] and the European Research and Development [R&D] team). In the various meetings we had with the CEO and the board at the beginning, we found that the representatives of the different groups had very distinct interests, with the consequence that our programme found widely differing degrees of support among them. The CEO, who had taken over responsibility for the European operations only recently and was expected by the Japanese headquarters (HQ) to "turn around" the business on the German market, found the programme to be a key component of his strategy. The Aftermarket unit had been operating in a very challenging market for a long time and lacked ideas on how to position themselves in their highly competitive environment. They hoped to gain new insights through a training programme and were consequently very open to it. In contrast, the OEM unit worked very closely with just two automobile companies for the most part and produced customised high-end electronic products for them. The staff in this department had responded poorly to growth in demand from the customer base and became chaotic in their organisation. Nevertheless, leaders had managed to evade facing up to their structural problems and attempted to master the situation with ever-greater workloads. The OEM board members' aversion to contemplating new ways of co-operation was reflected in their resistance towards our programme. The R&D representative was equally reluctant to send his managers to the programme, albeit for a different reason: his people were not affected by the business pressures that affected the OEM and the Aftermarket managers. Quite the opposite, R&D managers worked under much more moderate conditions which did not necessitate a change in current practices.

Starting slowly

We had been working very closely with the VP of HR Kubo san and his German HR manager Christine in the first three months to determine the concept of the programme. We knew that Christine's role was an administrative one as any decision-making power lay in the hands of her Japanese boss. Nevertheless, we met a couple of times and had several conference calls throughout the first months of our engagement, mainly to hear about the latest rumours about the programme. At one point, we needed Kubo san's opinion on how to move on, yet he was not available. He would neither answer phone calls nor e-mails. In addition, it was during this time that Christine decided to leave the company, so Gavin and I no longer had an unofficial informant. Surprisingly, after a month in which we had fruitlessly attempted to contact Kubo san, he called me up. He was very angry and complained about the way we had not taken any action in the interim. When I explained how diligently I had been trying (without success) to get in touch with him, things became even worse. He demanded a meeting to explore the situation.

When Gavin and I met Kubo san the following week, we found ourselves in a discussion which was very difficult for us to bear. I knew that I had tried to talk to him on several occasions and found myself being remonstrated for having failed to do exactly that. This meeting was also used to introduce Christine's successor, Carla. Although she was German, Carla had lived in Japan for almost a decade. She had been hired for her knowledge of Japanese culture and her Japanese language skills. She realised how Gavin and I were suffering in this meeting, and at some point she gave us non-verbal cues to restrain ourselves. When we stopped defending ourselves, Kubo san became more relaxed. He opened the window, took a seat on the windowsill and lit a cigarette. It was at this point that he revealed that the board had decided to conduct the programme, but that the costs should not be incurred in the current fiscal year. In a sense, he was doomed to wait until the end of the fiscal year while he wanted the programme to begin immediately. Since there was almost no money to spend at the moment, however, he did not know what to do.

When Gavin and I left, we both felt exhausted. Aside from the fact that the programme could not start as we had planned, we anticipated that overall co-operation could become very difficult when lack of knowledge of the Japanese culture on our part might complicate the programme in an unusual way.

As consultants, we did not question the process, but instead tried to help the CEO by giving advice on how to communicate properly, that is, what he should say in order to make people understand what the rationale and purpose behind his thinking was. By doing so, we hoped to overcome the resistance many managers within AAE seemed to feel. The fact that, like in other programmes of the same kind before, this procedure neither reduced employee's resistance nor fostered the emergence of aligned leadership behaviours has made me review my practice fundamentally, and that is why I want to propose a different way of understanding change in organisations.

Towards a new understanding of what happens to me at work

Despite the strategic importance our project was said to have and the client's enthusiasm about our consultancy work, struggles over budgets began to have an impact, ultimately revealing internal power asymmetries at the client organisation which caused such embarrassment for our direct interlocutors that they could not find a way to discuss the development of the situation openly. Highly conflictual conversations were the result, and eventually we consultants were embarrassed and blamed for not having interacted professionally. A multi-year programme was on the verge of being terminated before it had even started. Gavin and I went from being lionised to lacerated within a brief time span and found ourselves struggling in trying to make sense of what was going on. Nonetheless, we found a way to live with ambiguity and hostility and stayed engaged, apparently with more success than any of our competitors; we eventually became the sole provider for years of leadership development programmes for this organisation.

Since I could not find ways of exploring these experiences, ones which demonstrate the potential for shame, humiliation and exclusion, and the simultaneous experience of recognition and misrecognition in the orthodox management literature, I will draw on the theory of complex responsive processes of relating (e.g. Stacey et al., 2000; Griffin, 2002; Shaw, 2002; Stacey, 2007, 2010) and sociological theories of recognition (e.g. Hegel in Wood, 1990; Honneth, 1994, 2001) to make sense of my own practice from a different perspective.

As I will lay out below, these authors represent for me an understanding which takes recognition as a non-teleological concept; it does not serve any further end. It is a process through which we manifest or renegotiate our identity continuously through the encounter with the other, and this process cannot be managed.

On complex responsive processes of relating

The perspective of complex responsive processes thinking (Griffin, 2002; Shaw, 2002; Stacey 2007, 2010) offers me an approach which gives serious consideration to these paradoxical experiences of mine. It argues that global patterns – which are understood to be the organisation – arise through the multitude of local interactions among people, not because of the will of powerful individuals. In their local interaction, individuals negotiate the realisation of their intentions by enabling and constraining each other in relationships of power reflecting their current ideologies. Nevertheless, people have the ability to question modes of interaction, to be creative and to a degree recognise and critically reflect upon ideologies. It is these attributes which paradoxically at the same time allow for unanticipated change of habituated patterns of co-operation. Paradox here means that in human interaction, two contradictory processes are constantly open at the same time. In that way, global patterns of interaction emerge which no one single individual desired, and any form of interaction is paradoxically open to reiteration and change at the same time.

When individuals interact, they constantly act upon and respond to each other's desires and intentions. The aroused conflict is mediated by the fact that over the centuries, human communities have evolved social practices for the avoidance of overt violence in the face of conflicting intentions using mechanisms of internalised social rituals of courtesy, the experience of embarrassment and shame when these are violated and the fear of being excluded as a consequence (Elias, 1978). Since societal structures have become increasingly complex, the way people depend on one another has changed as well. Elias (ibid.) argues that our interdependency involves power relationships among us. But – and this is significant – even the most powerful depend on the recognition of the less powerful, since otherwise there would not be any experience of power and interdependency. In terms of complex responsive processes, the notion of an autonomous self is abandoned in favour of the concept of a social self where our identity arises in a dialectical process in which "I" and "me" (Mead, 1934), the sense of my individual agency and the way I experience how others perceive me are in a constant state of tension, and leave our identity continuously open for both perpetuation and redefinition.

On theories of recognition

Being dependent on the other also points to the notion of mutual recognition. In order to feel recognised, we need an "other." Hegel is the philosopher best known for having drawn attention to this aspect of human interrelating. In the interaction with another self-conscious human being, we experience a "certain mutuality, equality, even identity of ... desire and interest with that of the other ... that the other of which I am aware is myself – myself as other" (Wood, 1990: 86). Becoming aware of this mutuality is for Hegel the source from which self-consciousness arises, and he explains the underlying process with the shared desire for being recognised by the other (Hegel in Wood, 1990: 85).

In Germany, Axel Honneth has contributed significantly to our understanding of the dynamics of recognition. At the heart of Honneth's discussion about recognition is the gradually growing capacity of the individual to take into account others' positions and their desires. The individuation process coincides with an ever-expanding capacity of the individual to decentre and consequently to experience states of enlarged subjectivity (Honneth, 1994). Honneth believes that throughout this process, we are socialised, in that we voluntarily confine ourselves in our own desires in the face of the other, and this is ultimately, yet paradoxically, also a precondition for the experience of self-determination as well as a prerequisite for mutual recognition (Honneth, 2001: 100). The mature individual will have the capacity to become more detached, postpone desires and develop a language which connects him or her with others in such a way that they "relate positively" (ibid.: 87) and recognise others' needs as well as their own. This postponing is not felt to be restricting, however, "because if the other reciprocates in the same positive way this is experienced as true freedom" to act, that is self-determinacy (ibid.).

Such a view stands diametrically opposite to most management authors who conceptualise recognition as some form of technique (e.g. Daniels, 2000; Hansford, 2003; Gostick and Elton, 2007). Their intention – with quite a behavioural subtext – seems to be to teach managers how to recognise their employees properly and so ensure conformity with wider organisational rules, ultimately substituting organisational values for one's own ethical standards (see Willmott, 1993, for a critical appraisal).

Importantly, and I will devote more space to this in a later section, the experience of recognition and misrecognition cannot easily be separated. In fact, in the example I gave above, I experienced the paradox of being recognised and misrecognised at the same time, which affects positions of power, feelings of being in or out of the groups one participates in and the way one depends on others. In other words, the experience of being simultaneously recognised and misrecognised coincides at once with a feeling of being either included or excluded. In the vignette I presented, I pointed out the tension that Gavin and I experienced when we believed to be the recognised partner for a client, whilst at the same time being misrecognised when we found ourselves attacked and demoralised by that selfsame client for our inability to meet their demands. We felt like we were at the same time included in the group of those who worked together with the board and other senior stakeholders and excluded from that in-group as we were cut off from relevant decision-making processes.

Beyond the practice-theory split

Cultural change and leadership development initiatives are important aspects of renegotiating who we are and what we do in organisations. Such enterprises are anxiety- and resistance-provoking, because redefining the way we co-operate may profoundly affect our positions of power and our sense of identity. In my experience, people are also put under strain by the complex social processes involved. Managers quickly show resistance to programmes that aim at modifying their leadership behaviour according to guidelines set out by senior leaders. Often, executives tend to display differing degrees of agreement with such programmes, but not because they do not believe in their usefulness. Patterns of agreement and disagreement often reflect power struggles amongst executives which are rarely brought to consultants' attention early on, but which tend to have an impact on the programme throughout its execution. I gave an example of such dynamics previously where senior managers and board members at a client organisation struggled throughout the process of setting up a leadership programme because some feared power would tilt away from them as a consequence. After all, it is quite difficult – despite (or perhaps because of) well-intended goals and communicated agendas – to address the paradoxical experience of the continuously co-existing potential for sincerity and hypocrisy of those affected in highly political processes of culture change or leadership development programmes. Why is this difficult and why is it important anyway? It is difficult because these paradoxical dynamics are easily simplified so that we come to believe that we can manage them. It is important because believing that we can manage paradoxical processes, while constantly finding that actually we cannot, must have important ramifications for what I in my role as consultant can actually contribute or achieve in my work.

My previous belief in my ability to manage highly complex social processes is expressed in a way of thinking in which elements which are often self-contradictory are simplified by being split in a dualistic fashion (Stacey et al., 2000). Through the process of simplification, paradoxical dynamics are perceived in a "both ... and" fashion (Griffin, 2002), so they appear manageable in such a way that they can effectively be dealt with sequentially. With this dualistic split, the paradoxical tension which is, however, so much the daily experience of people who must be (ostensibly) sincere and (behind the scenes) hypocritical at the same time in order to survive the organisational-political game is lost. Splitting the paradoxical experience will allow us to talk rationally about what needs to be done. Yet, what such a split at once prevents is further exploration of seemingly irrational resistance and hypocrisy, which is nevertheless part of peoples' experience when officially they have to comply with an agenda for change, but at the same time fear that that change will jeopardise their reputation or position of power. In order to reach a more complex understanding of what is going on, I suggest attending to these different aspects of peoples' experience through inviting them to reflect upon the official agenda for change, their response to that agenda and also the strong feelings of resistance or denial this may call out in them.

I believe it is important to acknowledge that talking in dualisms effectively glosses over and reduces our otherwise kaleidoscopic everyday experience. For me, this experience is often conflictual and even paradoxical, and it is important to pay attention to these aspects precisely because they are at the heart of the radical contingency of our life in organisations. It is this latter aspect which has the capacity to heighten people's sensibility and to amplify feelings of vulnerability, which can fuel tendencies to resist or undermine change programmes.

I claim that much of the work I do as an organisation consultant does not deliver the intended results, because when I try to trivialise reality through simplistic, sequential multistep change agendas, I do not take seriously people's experience of this radical contingency. In fact, I have come to believe that the experience of contingency in their work actually deserves intensification, not simplification.

Over time, I have come to understand that my insights demand that I be radically open in my conversations with clients. What such openness requires of me is to resist clients' desires to depend on me as the "expert" who knows what form of leadership or communication needs to be applied. What I can nevertheless contribute is my ability to help clients to cope with the feelings of uncertainty which they inevitably encounter in the processes of organisational change. I may be recognised for being able to keep on exploring and so contribute to conversations which are usually absent from leadership development programmes, despite being fully aware that such form of inquiry might also lead clients to misrecognise me for not living up to generally accepted forms of organisational consulting. The potential for misrecognition is ever-present since there is no guarantee for the experience of uncertainty to be sufficiently mitigated. For sure, clients may develop a more complex understanding of their situation. They may become more realistic about what they can actually do about it, and as a result, they may develop a more sophisticated stance as they begin to understand what action they are capable of. Nevertheless, they may equally find the intensification of their experience, which includes feelings of uncertainty – and that I suggest as a way to develop a more realistic understanding – to be distressing. If the attempt to develop a more mature stance is successful, I will be recognised for my ability to further peoples' ability to come to terms with a challenging long-term outlook for their future. But if the attempt fails, I can easily become the scapegoat for making an already problematic situation even more difficult to bear. It is in the ability to tolerate the constant potential for being recognised and misrecognised at the same time as a consultant that I support my clients while negotiating what we think needs to be done.

On the notion of practical tools

My clients' obsession with "practical" tools, it seems to me, is in fact an expression of the dualistic mode of thought I have begun to disarticulate throughout this chapter. Clients I work for usually split theory and practice into discreet areas so that we have different conversations about how they think about their practice theoretically (planning) and what they do practically (implementation). The important insight gained through the perspective of complex responsive processes is that theory and practice are interlaced or in a dialectical state of tension where one would not exist without the other. Consequently, a dualistic mode of thought would actually inhibit my clients' ability to grapple with the often complex nature of their own experience when they try to put thought before action. The problems which arise out of the dualistic split between theory and practice have been explored most prominently by scholars in the tradition of American Pragmatism such as George H. Mead and John Dewey. They traced back the dualistic mode of thought to Descartes' insight that we can doubt everything except ourselves as the entity which does the doubting. This not only led to the split between mind (which doubts) and body (which can be doubted). More profoundly, it made one's own mind the only foundation from which any further understanding could emerge. The problem which results is precisely how we then come to understand and actually interact with other people when, in principle, we can doubt everything, including our relationship with them. Hence, American Pragmatists proposed that the Cartesian split does not exist in the first place because it simply does not reflect our experience. If we doubted everything, we would ultimately be paralysed because any action would be rendered meaningless. American Pragmatists criticised Descartes's conclusion for what it was: a conclusion gained through an isolated and highly abstract meditation about our position in the world. They suggested that thought and action cannot be split because thought, or the necessity to think, only arises in concrete action. Once we find ourselves in a new or a conflictual situation, our first response is not to doubt these circumstances, but to begin to think. So, thinking and acting always occur together, never separately (Joas and Knöbl, 2004: 186–191).

I suggest that it is in those moments when there is potential for recognition and misrecognition to paradoxically arise together that the experience of unsplit "thinking as acting" is most obvious. As exemplified by the vignette I presented earlier, consultants will likely find themselves in situations where they feel recognised and misrecognised at the same time. In my experience, it is the ability to tolerate, negotiate and reflect upon the inevitable tension which arises from such paradoxical situations that can put consultants in a position to explore further the options at hand. Often, there is partiality on the side of the consultant for collapsing that paradox to seek recognition through the introduction of tools or models. Instead, I am proposing trying to hold on to that paradox, that is, to not seek immediate recognition but to intervene in ways which may equally lead the consultant to be misrecognised. For example, when I invite clients to talk about the painful aspects of a change programme which seem unresolvable despite a grand vision or a clear purpose; or when we explore the implications of unexpressed political aspects that thwart our projects, but may be dangerous to address in the presence of powerful top managers; or when I encourage people to talk about their desire for concrete solutions and how they feel about me as the consultant who does not offer any obvious solutions. People may find such form of consulting helpful when I try to address latently simmering tensions and thereby broaden their perspective beyond the introduction of tools or models as much as they may find it to be a prolongation of their agony. Obviously, the outcome of such interaction cannot be predicted. That is what I mean by "hanging on to paradox" when I try to contribute to bringing about situations in which I may be recognised as much as I may be misrecognised. If consultants are able to bear such situations, it can put them in a unique position where their clients' experience begins to resonate with them. The consultant may be able to re-experience their clients' emotional state through paying attention to their own affective responses. Instead of promoting tools or techniques for change and so muting the resonance, I suggest consultants should use these emotional cues to stimulate or intensify further inquiry.[4] In my experience, such approach can mutually aid clients and consultants in evolving a more comprehensive understanding of their current situation.

I believe that many consultant interventions do not yield the intended outcome precisely because it can be utterly difficult and downright excruciating to sustain one's reflexive position in moments of heightened emotional or political pressure, not knowing if one will be recognised or misrecognised. It is much easier to split and collapse the paradox by turning to "best practices," tools or abstract models which promise recognition of the consultant's expertise and relief of such pressure for all involved. At once, the consultant's inability to bear the potential for misrecognition will foreclose an exploration of those social dynamics which only emerge under such pressure. Consequently, in putting an end to a possibly painful conversation, they simultaneously negate the opportunity to inquire into novel forms of interaction which may only be stimulated if we dare to explore what exactly makes such conversation so painful. The exploration I am suggesting may be important precisely because it is unmitigated by simplistic models; after all, such models are usually unmoored from clients' experience and do not reflect their complex reality.

I want to emphasise that I am not suggesting that there are times when it makes sense to try to intensify awareness of social dynamics and that there are other times when the application of models or tools is what is called for. Apparently, it is such splitting that I have argued against. Instead, I want to provide an alternative to the dualistic notion of the consultant's ability to oscillate between the "cognitive labour" of providing abstract models and being engaged in the "emotional labour" of making sense of what is going on in the social interaction. I am rather pointing to the concurrence of the consultant's cognitive ability to become aware of the variations of the intensity of the emotional labour they find themselves immersed in. From that perspective, one of the consultant's main tasks is to exercise practical judgement in relation to the affective cues they are becoming aware of, and to decide when it is time for asking probing questions, proposing interpretations of evolving patterns of interaction or remaining silent. It is in the exercise of this practical judgement that thinking and acting occur together simultaneously and spontaneously. Thinking does not come before acting and the object of thought is not abstract models, but the emotional content of the conversation consultants are taking part in. Again, I believe this to be important because, in my experience, such an approach can offer avenues for exploring what has exercised group members in the past, how this may be related to what matters most to them in their current situation and what reasonable next steps they are now becoming aware of, whereas the application of tools rather detracts and splits them from all these aspects. In my experience, it will usually lead into a rather stale conversation over how people need to learn how to use these tools which offer the promise of a life less complex but illusory or unsustainable.

Hence, it is this split, I claim, which explains consultants' and my clients' difficulty in understanding more clearly why the application of increasingly sophisticated concepts such as "Immunity to Change" (Kegan and Laskow Lahey, 2009) or why using tools for data-analytics to underpin culture change efforts are not terribly helpful in coming to terms with the dilemmas confronting them every day. These tools are responded to positively by many of my clients as they ostensibly simplify our otherwise complex experience. Instead of trying to simplify their experience, my response to my insight would be to intensify the experience and by working into this dialectical tension of "thinking as acting," helping clients to find the courage to express what is actually going on for them instead of resorting to sophisticated tools that only serve to draw abstract conclusions from their experience. As a result, I have begun to resist idealised notions as to what becomes possible through the application of this or that tool in lieu of potentially opening up further conversations.

Towards implications for my practice

My goal in OD interventions has changed insofar as I have begun to coax clients to pay attention to the multifacetedness of their daily experience which quite often leads to discussions concerning conflict, organisational politics or struggles for recognition. However, I in no way point them in one direction or the other, but I do not block exploration into these realms either. As the focus of my attention has shifted, I have seen changes in my work which are at once subtle and significant. One important aspect which I have noticed is this: I remind myself repeatedly that I will not have any single "right" answer, but that all I can do is help people reflect upon what they do in particular situations. Sometimes I raise their awareness of patterns they are enacting, which can then become a moment of greater insight for all involved. Over time, I have tried to intensify this experience, and I have become aware that reinterpreting my work in this way has enabled me to come to terms with the fact that there is no guarantee of "greater insight" to be gained as well. Tolerating this element of unpredictability allows me to encourage clients to explore aspects of their practice, which typically remained unaddressed. One important consequence of working in this spirit for me is this: I do not try to work towards a concrete solution, if by solution we mean a point at which everybody knows what needs to be done to start working now. Having said that, such an approach may trigger aggression just as easily because participants may begin to doubt the value of my work if we near the end of a session and no concrete action planning has been resolved. Working under these conditions speaks about my ability as consultant to endure the constant possibility of being recognised and misrecognised. I believe this is a rarely addressed aspect of the work of a consultant, but one which is crucial as it helps my clients to develop a more realistic notion of what it is that we are capable of achieving. It may also support my clients in honing their ability to think critically about their own practice once my assignment has come to an end.

Processes of recognition: a paradoxical understanding

Part of the paradoxical view I am suggesting is that a feeling of being recognised only arises through exposing oneself constantly to the risk of being misrecognised. Only when we interact with others do we create the conditions under which others may take our views seriously, that is, recognise us, and vice versa. Nevertheless, any exchange may just as well highlight our differences from others, potentially leading us into conflict.

I understand the ability to tolerate the potential for misrecognition and conflict to be an important characteristic of organisation consultants, and I have argued that such ability is rarely addressed in the dominant literature on management consulting. The idea is more that consultancy knowledge is generic and that it can be applied in many situations in which clients may find themselves. It is the task of the consultant to convey their expertise in order to bring about a shared understanding among managers and employees, so that all work in step towards the desired vision for the future, almost regardless of the contingency of contexts (e.g. Cockman et al., 1999; Schein, 1999/2009; Kofman, 2006).

I have drawn on the discourse of complex responsive processes thinking (Griffin, 2002; Shaw, 2002; Stacey, 2007) and theories of recognition to develop a different understanding. As an important consequence, I have tried to describe how consultants experience entanglement in the nexus of power relationships and I have presented these dynamics as processes of recognition. In particular, I have conceptualised the fluctuation of power relationships – the political – as the potential for the paradoxical experience of being recognised and misrecognised at the same time. Acting politically may cause people to demonstrate conformity with official statements and demands in public, but to behave quite differently in private. It seems to me that this experience is quite common in particular for consultants who are working on bringing about change, and the narrative I presented gives an example from an organisational context that supports this view. The interaction which follows from such behaviour often presents people with a precarious experience which they find difficult to address. I have argued that such phenomena are closely related to activities which those in power utilise in their attempt to sustain a given hegemonic order, for example, when in the narrative I presented earlier, all board members ostensibly supported the setting up of a new leadership development programme, while behind the scenes those who represented the OEM and R&D business opposed the programme and worked against its coming into being. In this light, processes of recognition enhance our understanding of how and why power relationships are reiterated or why they fluctuate.

The above narrative on the difficult beginnings of a leadership development programme is a prime example of such a case. Internal power struggles undermined a project which was otherwise deemed to be of the highest strategic importance. This left us consultants fairly powerless when we were confronted with the unexpected postponement of the programme, even though we were officially contracted by the CEO to deliver. Once into the programme, we learned that senior managers constantly faced struggles of this nature, and now they were asking us, the consultants, for clear advice about operating in this context, even though we had just experienced ourselves how easily we could become paralysed as well.

Stacey (2007), picking up on the ideas of Elias (1970), argues that when people interrelate, they have to justify their actions in some way or another to others, which consequently can constrain as well as enable their actions. This is how power relations define our dependency on one another. Often, a power relationship is marked by an asymmetry in which the need of one party for the other is greater than in the opposite direction. But this need is always open to fluctuation, and the less powerful will never be completely powerless since "the power of the more powerful depends upon the recognition of the less powerful that this is indeed so" (Griffin, 2002: 352). Such understanding has important ramifications for what we think consultants do and are actually capable of achieving because it indicates that the way recognition is conceptualised in the dominant literature on management is much too simple. This is problematic since in this discourse it is perfectly rational to believe that managers or consultants have the capacity to shape actively the conditions under which employees can be intentionally motivated and this be the prerequisite for successful change programmes or realisation of long-term strategies. One important aspect in this tradition of thought is that proper recognition of employees will foster alignment of many, make all feel included as well as contribute to avoidance of conflict, eventually yielding better bottom line results (e.g. Peters, 1988; Kofman, 2006; Gostick and Elton, 2007).

Over time, I have come to question this rationality, and I would part from the above authors on three points. First, my ideas do not point in the direction of "using" recognition as a technique to motivate and control employees. Such an understanding would rest on a cognitivist approach which puts the rationally acting individual at the centre; it leaves out the social and relational aspects of human interaction, that is, political behaviour, the experience of shame or embarrassment and dynamics of inclusion and exclusion. All these experiences arise only in social contexts, and no manager or consultant can determine precisely which responses they might call out in others. Consequently, I do not think that recognition can be used as a tool because the experience of recognition is never unidirectional.

Second, and as a consequence, I am not suggesting that consultants' main task is to realise solutions or to bring about uniformly shared agreement among their clients about proceeding. While such understanding is very much at the heart of what most management thinkers and consultants advocate, I propose that consultants should not try to bring about alignment or harmony, but that they take diversity and conflict seriously. This might help to understand why change programmes fail or why "best practices" cannot easily be transferred from one work context to another. The experience of otherness (and its corollary diversity) is an important aspect of the human encounter, and denying or attempting to manage diversity seems virtually impossible. This is my reason for advocating the exact opposite: resisting the desire to manage difference or diversity and acknowledging that most efforts to align human interaction have rarely been successful.

Third, I am advocating an approach which does not try to do away with paradox. I would argue instead that human interaction is often paradoxical and that there is no way of overcoming this paradoxicality. I would describe the paradox of recognition in this way: recognition means seeing the other as human (like me) and at the same time recognising that the other is different (unlike me) because of this humanity. Starting from this premise, consultants or managers might begin to perceive their own practice differently. Realising that we can at the same time experience being similar and different, being recognised and misrecognised, or being included and excluded may be difficult to understand, but even more difficult to bear. Nevertheless, the daily experience of organisational consultants is often contradictory, and they often turn to an idealised understanding of what managers or consultants can do as a way to cope with that experience. In the writings of Hegel, Stacey et al. and others, I have found a different way to make sense of such experience, one which does not deny contradiction or ascribe heroic abilities to consultants but which encourages them to pay close attention to observe what is actually going on when people co-operate and compete in organisations. This demands a change in attitude and expectations as to what consultants can do. Such a shift would require them to be radically open and to encourage their clients to keep on exploring the often contradictory circumstances they are operating under. There would be no single solution to this or that problem. The idea of "a solution" is redefined to be rather a prolonged process of complexifying and paying attention to one's experience without seeking a final destination, a continuous intensifying in experiencing one's interactions which might best be expressed as the constant existence of potential to find new forms of co-operation without having a guarantee that this actually happens.

Conclusion

I understand it to be my responsibility to reflect critically on my practice and not simply to accept what is given and thought possible in my work, to find ways to challenge the prevailing hegemonic order of management consultancy. The necessity to do so arises for me out of the inferior explanations this discourse offers for the phenomena I experience in my work. To offer a critique in this context means exploring the contemporary conditions of the dominant discourse and the way it becomes manifest in our daily work so that I can uncover its unquestioned basic assumptions. However, the subversive element in the managerialist discourse is that people who speak its language easily hinder exactly this: the possibility to protest, to explore difference and otherness, effectively preventing the articulation of alternative forms of making sense. The emerging discourse on the concept of diversity and inclusion is a case in point. Instead of realising that the "inclusion" only makes sense if you think "exclusion" at the same time, there is a tendency to collapse this paradox through simple statements about the importance of "inclusion." Pointing to the one-sidedness of this idealised perspective ironically tends to call out responses that effectively prevent the exploration of a more diversified and inclusive understanding.

Nevertheless, I must acknowledge that the way people speak about their activities is an important part of their identity, and by pointing out the inconsistencies of what they say, I might easily be perceived as someone who unduly complicates already complex modes of work. I might even risk being excluded from the field of consultancy, and if I want to support clients in becoming more detached about their practice, I must live with the anxiety this may arouse. Then, too, my insights oblige me to resist substituting one dominant view for another. My proposal is simply another perspective on my work, which I offer here as a viewpoint, which is more congruent with reality than those I find in the orthodox management canon. What is it that makes the view I present here more congruent with reality?

In my experience, catchphrases which have gained prominence in the dominant management discourse, are expressed by calls for more aligned forms of leadership and for reduced sets of competencies which everyone needs to develop and for widely shared organisational values which are to guide every individual's behaviour, all of which are actually attempts to mitigate difference. To me, such forms of simplification are an important reason why we are so often surprised when we discover that our projects do not go according to plan and life does not seem to co-operate.

To encounter some form of otherness is in my opinion not only inevitable in human interaction, but is actually the prerequisite for co-operation and the eventual emergence of the new. If there were no other, no differentiation in the form of "us" and "them" and if there were no constant negotiation about power and struggles for recognition, there would be no conflict neither would there be any (r)evolution. What I have sought to advocate is to pay attention to the generative tension which arises from such diversity as opposed to attempts to manage it. In my attempts to make sense of this experience, I have begun to take seriously the unpredictability that characterises human interaction and the way it serves to enable and constrain us.

Being enabled and constrained only appears as dualistic once we come to interpret interdependency with others as constraint in conflict with our intentions. One important consequence of this thought is that I and others are antagonistic poles which would, in turn, reinforce an individual notion of self. I have attempted to go beyond this notion by presenting a position which suggests that the experience of identity does not take place until we encounter the difference the other brings, because it is only through their (sometimes unexpected) responses to our gestures that we understand who we are. This is the process I have described as mutual recognition. The debate with the other provides us with the paradoxically co-existing experience of enablement and constraint. In other words, if there were no conflicting views, there would be no necessity to act and subsequently no experience of agency. As a consequence, I have argued that sameness and difference exist in dialectical tension rather than antagonistic opposition. The important social function of constraints, the experience of (inter-) dependency, is that they simultaneously order our experience and oblige us to co-operate. Action becomes our attempt to reflect and negotiate the responses we call out in others in the process of intermingling intentions. Such a notion helps us to transcend the practice/theory split since our necessity to think arises only if concrete action is called for; thought cannot come before action, both arise together.

Even though I find myself often called in to contribute to the management of social process, it seems virtually impossible for me to somehow know in advance how to best "manage" this or how to create spheres which are free of conflict and where thought is aligned because we all live and act in the same multiplicity of contexts which influence our intentions, in turn constrained and enabled through our exchange.

Such reflection must inevitably lead to different forms of struggle: I must be politic in my actions with colleagues and supervisors to ensure my survival in the highly competitive environment of a globally operating consulting firm. I must be very careful in sharing my doubts about the usefulness of the concepts and tools we employ. By the same token, I need to be very careful to appear neither hypocritical nor heretical in front of clients who ask for delivery of programmes based on a logic I am questioning. So what is left to me? After all, I need to find ways to communicate with others where I am recognised for the contributions I make, but can still recognise myself.

One credible option I see for myself is to participate in the groups my assignments take me to in such a way that I continue to explore even when the general tendency is to close down a conversation and "get to work."

The ideological stance behind this idea would be to "make better sense of the situation." I think that regardless of the group's context, my main contribution would be related to my ability to tolerate the struggle which "making better sense" may provoke and I believe that this is what colleagues and clients recognise in me. Negotiating and thinking processes can be experienced as action, and the only way, it seems to me, for practicing OD consultants to express this insight in their work and so to recognise themselves is by offering provisional viewpoints of how best to appropriate their present understanding in this or that context and inviting clients and colleagues to do the same. I do not propose definitive solutions, just awareness of contingency and radical openness; yet, this may turn out to be solution enough.

Notes

1 This chapter presents work that was first explored in the author's 2012 doctoral thesis entitled "An Exploration of Processes of Mutual Recognition in Organization Development Initiatives from the Standpoint of a Practising Consultant," available at https://uhra.herts.ac.uk/handle/2299/7658?show=full.
2 OEM business is marked by high volume business transactions with large key clients for whom customised products are designed.
3 The Aftermarket business unit is responsible for the development and distribution of end-consumer products.
4 In the volume on Leadership within this series, Flinn makes a similar point in his chapter's section "Dicks getting in the way of dialogue" when he contends than "rather than denying or suppressing our emotions we should learn to work with them."

References

Cockman, P., Evans, B., and Reynolds, P. (1999) *Consulting for Real People: A Client-Centred Approach for Change Agents and Leaders*, Maidenhead: McGraw-Hill.
Daniels, A.C. (2000) *Other People's Habits: How to Use Positive Reinforcement to Bring Out the Best in People Around You*, New York: McGraw-Hill.
Elias, N. (1970) *What Is Sociology?* New York: Columbia University Press.

Elias, N. (1978) *The Civilizing Process: Sociogenetic and Psychogenetic Investigations*, Oxford: Blackwell.

Gostick, A. and Elton, C. (2007) *The Carrot Principle: How the Best Managers Use Recognition to Engage Their People, Retain Talent, and Accelerate Performance*, New York: Free Press.

Griffin, D. (2002) *Emergence of Leadership*, London: Routledge.

Hansford, D. (2003) *The Magic of Employee Recognition: 10 Proven Tactics from CalPERS and Disney*, Scottsdale: WorldatWork.

Hegel, G. (1977) 'Phenomenology of Spirit' in Wood, A.W. (1990) *Hegel's Ethical Thought*, Cambridge: Cambridge University Press.

Honneth, A. (1994) *Kampf um Anerkennung*, Frankfurt: Suhrkamp.

Honneth, A. (2001) *Leiden an Unbestimmtheit*, Stuttgart: Reclam.

Joas, H. and Knöbl, W. (2004) *Sozialtheorie: Zwanzig einführende Vorlesungen*, Frankfurt a. M.: Suhrkamp.

Kegan, R. and Laskow Lahey, L. (2009) *Immunity to Change: How to overcome It and Unlock the Potential of Yourself and Your Organization*, Boston, MA: Harvard Business Press.

Kofman, F. (2006) *Conscious Business: How to Build Value through Values*, Boulder, CO: Sounds True.

Mead, G.H. (1934) *Mind, Self and Society*, Chicago, IL: University of Chicago Press.

Peters, T.J. (1988) in Willmott, H. (1993) (ed) 'Strength is Ignorance; Slavery is Freedom: Managing Culture in Modern Organizations', *Journal of Management Studies*, 30(4): 515–552.

Schein, E.H. (1999/2009) *The Corporate Culture Survival Guide*, San Francisco, CA: Jossey-Bass.

Shaw, P. (2002) *Changing Conversations in Organizations: A Complexity Approach to Change*, Oxon: Routledge.

Stacey, R. (2007) *Strategic Management and Organisational Dynamics*, Harlow: Pearson Education.

Stacey, R. (2010) *Complexity and Organizational Reality*, Oxon: Routledge.

Stacey, R., Griffin, D., and Shaw, P. (2000) *Complexity and Management: Fad or Radical Challenge to Systems Thinking?*, Oxon: Routledge.

Willmott, H. (1993) 'Strength is Ignorance; Slavery is Freedom: Managing Culture in Modern Organizations', *Journal of Management Studies*, 30(4): 515–552.

Wood, A.W. (1990) *Hegel's Ethical Thought*, Cambridge: Cambridge University Press.

4

ACTUALISING PLURALITY

AN ARENDTIAN PERSPECTIVE ON RESPONDING TO POWERLESSNESS AND LOSS OF FREEDOM

Karina Solsø

Introduction

When I entered the field of organisational development some years back, I held the view that rising through the organisational hierarchy as a manager meant increasing the degree of autonomy and freedom. Now that I work with some of those senior managers as a consultant I am struck by the naivety of that assumption. What I have found is quite the opposite: becoming more senior means increasingly being tied. Tied in interdependent relationships, tied by expectations formed through the history of an organisation and tied by a discourse on management which simultaneously enables and constrains one's practice (Stacey & Mowles, 2016).

In this chapter, I will draw attention to a particular kind of ties, namely the ties that arise from the rational and instrumental thinking that dominate management theory and practice, and which managers are obliged to take up in order to be seen as competent and worthy of inclusion in the powerful elite of an organisation (ibid.). One of the ways in which this pattern reveals itself is through the rational and instrumental thinking that managers rely upon when they engage in conversations about problems in their joint work. It is a kind of thinking which excludes emotional, relational and political aspects of the problems (Townley, 2008).

Having been socialised and trained to think in instrumental rational ways about the causes of and the solutions to such problems, it can be a struggle to create public forums within which people can engage with the aspects of the problems that have to do with relationships and conflicting views of the good (Shaw, 2002). In my experience, this can lead to attempts at creating solutions to problems, which fail to be fruitful. If this happens over and over again, this can slowly lead to a sense of powerlessness when it comes to trusting the capacity to engage with the problem in a way that can lead to more helpful practices. What is left is a sense of lack of political freedom (Taylor, 1991) and self-efficacy (Rosa, 2016) in influencing one's situation.

This chapter inquires into such powerlessness and loss of freedom. Speaking about feeling powerless as a manager is often not a part of the public conversations in organisations. Such painful thoughts and feelings are often only disclosed in conversations with trusted colleagues or friends behind closed doors, because being in such roles typically requires subscribing to a discourse of positivity and optimism (Ehrenreich, 2010; Brinkmann, 2017). This discourse of optimism can itself strengthen a feeling of incompetence and loneliness as a manager or consultant. In my experience qualities of interaction like powerlessness and loss of meaning are present in large organisations to a degree that warrants attention and reflection. What is it about our ways of engaging with each other in organisational settings, which leads to these feelings? What are the forms of practice and thinking involved? What are the consequences of this pattern? And finally, what might be ways of responding to the ongoing flow of interaction that can allow for the experience of meaning and freedom?

I will explore these questions by drawing on a concrete experience from my practice as a consultant. Following a narrative description of this example, I will theorise around these questions drawing primarily on the work of the philosopher and political thinker Hannah Arendt, who took an interest in the question of the way in which the rise of bureaucratic thinking had powerful implications for our sense of freedom.

I will argue that:

- The dominance of an instrumental rational discourse in organisations has marginalised conversations that emphasise the relational and political aspects of interaction;
- The marginalising of a relational and political discourse can lead to managers experiencing powerlessness and loss of freedom;
- Hannah Arendt's idea of 'actualising plurality' holds the potential of temporal achievements of a fragile 'we' within which it is possible to experience meaningfulness and freedom;
- Consultants can play a role in actualising plurality through collaborating with clients to try to create public realms for reflective exploration and debate.

The contribution of this chapter is (1) an analysis of a contemporary malaise of management practice, which leads to powerlessness and loss of freedom for managers, and (2) an attempt at describing a form of consultancy practice, which can offer a meaningful and promising way forward for managers working in large corporations.

Narrative: powerlessness and loss of freedom

I sat a little restless in my chair as we began the seminar for the extended management group consisting of 18 managers. This was the third seminar I facilitated for this group of managers working in an IT company. In my conversations with John, the director of the management team, prior to this seminar, it had become clear that they were struggling with establishing an effective enough sense of collaboration and responsibility between them. John wanted to spend the seminar dealing with this issue.

John opened the seminar in an unusually serious tone, saying that whilst he was well aware that all the managers had been working really hard and had been doing so for months, he was beginning to feel that there were things that simply weren't good enough, things that had to be done differently. An immediate tension materialised in the group. John continued saying that too often they faced situations where problems fell in between stools and what remained was a tendency for nobody to really feel an urgency to do something about the things that desperately needed attention.

He said that I had given him the task of writing a story about an example of this as a way of opening up a conversation about this theme. He looked to me and I said a few sentences about how we would start this seminar with John reading his story and them sharing their thoughts about it. The ambition, I said, was to try and come to a deeper understanding of the pattern that John talked about in order for them as a collective to be able to do something about it. John began reading. The story centred on the disappointment and embarrassment that he continued to feel when thinking about the budgeting process, an area of their responsibility, which in his view had failed for the second year in a row. He described how over and over again they had been surprised by unexpected costs of deals with clients, which they hadn't been aware of, and which had become evident only very late.

Despite the fact that everybody in the room seemingly knew about the problems with the budgeting process, there was a sense of surprise hanging in the air. Perhaps the surprise was due to the sudden airing of dirty laundry that was normally kept in shadowy corners. Perhaps they were surprised by John speaking about his own emotions in the context of the budget. As John finished his reading, the managers were staring down at the floor and nobody really knew how to move on from there. John himself looked intimidated by the silence.

I asked them what thoughts John's story provoked for them. It took a while before anybody was ready to say something. Henrik, a senior manager, broke the silence: he said that he sat with a feeling of embarrassment. Others nodded. Rebecca, another manager who had been working in the company for a while, continued by making the point that she also found it embarrassing that this had happened twice in a row, but to be honest, she couldn't see how they could change this, because there are so many stakeholders and processes involved which do not seem to be aligned. Paul, who was directly involved with the budget and who therefore probably felt somewhat attacked by John's story, continued:

> as soon as we think we are in control, the directors and managers from the development organisation overrule the agreed process and submit items to the budget, which should have been clear months back – they make

the case that we should know about these things, but we don't have the proper process or systems to do this work together.

Other managers continued in the same line of reflection drawing attention to the lack of clarity of responsibility and accountability.

A sense of failure, embarrassment and an emergent realisation of the complexity and the many interdependencies instilled a sense of hopelessness. Kenneth, who had been working in the company for many years, said that it felt like an exploration of the big disease of this company: a lack of power to execute. He said that thinking about doing something about that pattern made him feel powerlessness. They had tried so many times to do something about this, and here they were once again facing the same pattern. Silence emerged again and some of them looked at me. I sensed that they were expecting me to tell them how to get on from there.

I felt uncertain about what to do, and found myself summing up what I had heard and sharing a bit of my own thoughts as well. I said that I was noticing two patterns in the reflections. One rested on a notion of a well-functioning machine: it is the idea that if only the right procedures, the right systems, the right descriptions of roles and responsibilities were in place, then there would be better chances that they could make it work. The other pattern was about people outside this room: if only the people outside this room would do their work properly and align with the agreed decisions, then they would not have these problems. John took over, saying that for him the problems couldn't be solved through focusing on procedures, tools and role descriptions. It was about exercising leadership, taking action and getting the relevant stakeholders involved whenever needed and whenever a gap in understanding constrained them from acting in a coordinated way.

I watched the managers as he spoke. Most of them nodded, but I couldn't quite get my head around the quality of the nodding. My immediate sense of it was that they could see his point, but something more was going on. Was there a performative quality to this nodding? I was beginning to wonder if they were holding something back – whether something was going on that was hard to talk about. I was also beginning to think about whether they could tolerate the open-endedness and uncertainty of this conversation. It was time for a break. I said that I was sure that if these issues had been easy to fix, they would have done so already, and that in my view, the most promising way forward was to stay in the inquiry for a bit longer, which could hopefully allow us to understand more of the dynamics. They looked convinced enough by this and we took a break.

Making sense of the story

The conversation that emerged as a response to John's story was flavoured by a sense of disappointment and embarrassment. Looking back at the failed budget, the managers agreed that their collective effort hadn't been good enough. The process of reflecting on the experience added to the disappointment – leading to a shared sense of powerlessness and hopelessness.

In my experience, there was a sense of what Charles Taylor (1991) describes as *fragmentation*, which arises when people come to see themselves atomistically and less bound to others in joint projects and allegiances. What materialises is people being 'increasingly less capable of forming a common purpose and carrying it out' (ibid.:112). The managers shared the experience of embarrassment and frustration, but they didn't share a sense of capacity to do something about it. The room felt empty of imagination and initiative.

Expressions of hopelessness and powerlessness are not rare in my consultancy experience; particularly in large corporations, there is often a sense of frustration about problems that seem unsolvable despite various attempts at trying to do something about them. In reflecting on this sense of fragmentation and the seeming lack of capacity to form a common purpose and carry it out, one of the things that strikes me is the tendency to make sense of the budget problem through a highly rational and instrumental form of thinking. In a way, this is understandable. John's story was one of failure, and despite all enthusiastic talk about the potential for learning in such conversations, it is bound to raise the question: who is responsible? Or to put it more negatively: who is to blame? The conversation about responsibility quickly became a question about whether the right procedures, processes and tools were in place and whether those were implemented and used effectively. The complex phenomenon of a budget involving many interdependent people with divergent tasks and agendas was turned into a question of simple chains of means and ends.

In the following, I draw on the work of Hannah Arendt to explore the connection between this instrumental rational way of thinking and the hopelessness and powerlessness that the managers express.

Responsibility as following rules

Though at a very different and much more tragic scale, disappointment, powerlessness and hopelessness were also qualities of interaction permeating the context of the development of Hannah Arendt's political and philosophical ideas. Arendt was a German Jew who survived the Holocaust, and a political theorist and a philosopher inspired by Martin Heidegger and Karl Jaspers. Her experience of the Second World War became the most important context of her work, as she subsequently spent her life working on the questions that arose out of that experience.

One of the questions she dealt with was about how something so terrible as the Holocaust could happen. Through her analysis, she developed the argument that the Holocaust could only happen because of the rise of bureaucratic thinking throughout modernity (Arendt, 1973). One of the routes into that point was her inquiry into the trial of Adolph Eichmann (Arendt, 1963). Eichmann was a high-ranking officer with formal responsibility for the logistics of mass deportation of Jews to ghettos and extermination camps during the Second World War. When he went through his trial and was held responsible for his deeds, he famously argued that all he had done was to 'obey orders', he had 'done his duty'. Arendt was struck by Eichmann's explanation, by the absence of guilt or hatred towards the Jews, but perhaps mostly by the apparent inability to think about responsibility outside the category of rules.

This experience made Arendt reflect on the notion of responsibility. She refused to accept the idea that humans can take refuge from responsibility for their actions through appeals to ideologies that replace the human capacity for thinking and judgement with (bureaucratic) orders, rules and procedures (Arendt, 1963, 1973). She links this tendency to understanding responsibility as rules or procedures to the rise of bureaucratic thinking, and she argued that with modernity, people came to understand politics in terms of rules of government, in terms of administration. For Arendt, however, humans are not primarily rule-following creatures but political creatures, insofar as we have the capacity to think and to carry out our judgements through political acting and speaking (Arendt, 1958).

These observations resonate well with a dominant theme in the way the managers at the seminar made sense of the failed budget. The problems were interpreted to be administrative ones: insufficient processes and procedures and lack of clarity around deadlines and responsibility. Underneath this way of making sense of the situation was the assumption of instrumental rationality, which turns complex phenomena into chains of means and ends (Stacey, 2012): that if only the procedures, roles, processes and tools are well managed, then they would not have to spend time dealing with this budget problem. It would be fixed. But how did we come to understand such problems through an instrumental rational way of thinking?

Labour, work and action

Arendt's critical reflections on rule-following and bureaucratic thinking made her distinguish between three different forms of fundamental human activity: labour, work and action (Arendt, 1958).

Labour corresponds to the biological process of the human body. Labour as such is all the routinised activities that we do every day as biological beings. Those are activities like sleeping, eating, cooking, activities that have to do with the life cycle, and the human condition of labour is *life*.

Work corresponds to the artificial world of objects and has to do with fabrication and production. It is through 'working' that we produce things like, for example, buildings and furniture, which can outlast our own single lives. In a management context, the activity of 'work' is, for example, the fabrication of systems, procedures and tools which are intended to outlast our individual lives within an organisation. Whereas temporality within labour is the life cycle, *work* has its own man-made temporality with a beginning and an end. The basic condition of work is *the world*, and this space is dominated by the category of means and ends and functions through effective instrumental thinking.

The third of the three fundamental activities is *action*, which corresponds to the human condition of plurality. Action has to do with what goes on between people. Action is about speaking and acting politically, and it is through this showing up in the space of appearance that we become unique persons. Action is the most important of these categories to Arendt, as:

> a life without speech and without action, on the other hand ... is literally dead to the world; it has ceased to be a human life because it is no longer lived among men.
>
> (Arendt, 1958:187)

Following this, it is only through engaging in the activity of political action that we can take responsibility for what is done in our name.

The degradation of action in favour of work

It is the distinction between work and action that is relevant here in order for us to get closer to the question about how problems like a failed budget has come to be interpreted as a question of insufficient procedures and rules.

According to Arendt, one of the major changes that happened throughout modernity was that the conversational arenas for debating plural opinions were increasingly marginalised (Arendt, 1958, 1963). In the name of efficiency, problems that involve a plurality of perspectives and opinions were increasingly dealt with through implementation of administrative procedures that could solve the case through effective and reliable processes.

This argument resonates with the rise of a discourse on management rooted in disembedded and disembodied thinking (Townley, 2008). Economic, bureaucratic and technocratic approaches are seen to be effective because of the appeal to certainty and predictability. The inherent uncertainty that arises from human interaction is eliminated through these discourses (Stacey, 2012).

When the managers at the seminar talk about their budget problem through the concepts of unclear processes and procedures, lack of clarity around roles and responsibility and lack of the required systems, it can indeed be seen as an example of exactly what Arendt was talking about. Problems that arise as a consequence of a plurality of perspectives are dealt with administratively. The obvious example is the idea about mandate, which came up at the seminar. In most business contexts that I work in, mandates are thought about in administrative terms: a mandate is often simplistically thought about as a reification of authority, as something that can be handed over and something which – if it is clearly defined and agree upon – won't involve problems. However, from the numerous heated conversations in organisations about the complexity of mandates, it is clear that the social world is more complex, and that what we call mandate is an ongoing negotiation where people with different interests and viewpoints engage with each other in their attempt at achieving something. However, the formal conception of mandate doesn't involve this temporal and often conflictual nature of these processes.

As such, I suggest that Arendt's diagnosis of modernity as the marginalising of action in favour of work is resonant with the mood at the seminar expressed by the managers. But why was Arendt so critical of this development? What are the problematic consequences of the rise of instrumental rationality and thinking about politics in terms of administration?

Implications for a dominance of instrumental rationality

Several authors writing about organisation and management have dealt with the question of the consequences of a dominance of instrumental rationality, and they draw attention to a variety of implications. Flyvbjerg (2001) points to a lack of capacity to consider the importance of context, Townley (2008) draws attention to the marginalising of institutional, contextual, embodied and temporal aspects of what it means to act reasonably, Griffin (2002) argues that the notion of ethics is conceived in a limited way and Stacey & Mowles (2016) highlight the absence of a capacity to pay attention to the lived interaction between people.

Staying with a focus on Arendt's ideas here, a key aspect to dwell on is a question about the 'we' and the 'who' that arises out of a dominance of 'work' at the expense of 'action' (Loidolt, 2019). In other words, in what ways is it possible to show up as a politically acting individual in a context dominated by instrumental rationality?

In a 'community of producers', the appearance of the 'who' is banished to the private realm while economic interests dominate the public sphere. The unique identity and opinion of the acting individual is seen as irrelevant (Arendt, 1958). Consequently, a kind of 'we' emerges that is characterised by a certain lack of relatedness to others. In such a community, speech can easily become 'idle talk' and action can be degraded to mere accomplishment (ibid.).

These descriptions give words to the mood that I experienced at the seminar. It felt to me that what emerged from the responses of the managers can be seen as 'idle talk'. Nobody dared to show up with a unique identity and opinion, and this implicit denial of the significance of individuality plays a key role in construction of a pattern of 'work' rather than of 'action'. The Arendt scholar Sohie Loidolt links powerlessness and isolation to the experience of participating in a community of producers. She makes the point that finding ourselves staring into the same screens, allowing ourselves to be imprisoned in the subjectivity of our own singular experience, rather than participating with our own lively voice through political action, we can come to suffer from this lack of relatedness, which increase the sense of isolation (Loidolt, 2019:227).

Drawing on this line of argumentation, I want to make the argument that the experience of powerlessness and loss of freedom can be seen as a consequence of the marginalising of a relational and political discourse. A dominance of instrumental rationality leads to a community of producers where management practice is conceived through the category of work, namely as fabrication and administration of systems, procedures and tools, rather than being about speaking and acting in the public realm. The 'we' that arises is a producing we, where one is qualified due to the capacity to get things done rather than as showing up with a unique individuality. The 'producing we' is one of interchangeable units of production, spaces on organisation charts, while the 'political we' recognises the moral importance of individuals. What gets lost is the freedom, meaning and sense of responsibility that can arise from showing up as a 'who' in acting politically.

This argument leads to another question, because how might it be possible to respond to the emergent situation in a way that can allow for the emergence of a different kind of 'we'?

Narrative continued: disruption of stuckness

After the break, I asked the managers if any of them had examples that demonstrate similar patterns to the one we had explored together around John's story. Patterns around a lack of capacity to execute, patterns where they feel an inability to succeed as a collective, patterns where they feel a sense of powerlessness and hopelessness. After a bit of silence, Thomas, one of the well-established managers in the group, volunteered to give an example. Thomas's example centred on collaboration with managers in a different unit. He described the experience of participating in a project, which had become a disaster because they had realised some major problems very late in the process. In hindsight, he could see that he should have intervened earlier, and he gave the example of a meeting where he had stayed silent in a situation where he felt quite critical about the decisions that were about to be made. He had held back because he sat with some doubt in that meeting. He had already been quite critical towards his colleagues at the meeting, and finally, the director of the unit, Benjamin, seemed to have made up his mind already – so what was the point of insisting? In the end – he said – he didn't have the mandate to insist. In hindsight, however, he could see that this was exactly an example of the same pattern – a lack of following things through, which leads to a sense of failure and embarrassment.

The story resonated with several colleagues who had had similar difficulties. It led to reflections of problems related to the governance structure and the lack of clarity of the processes. One of the managers made the point that as long as it isn't clear that it is also a part of Thomas's formal role and responsibility to make the right decisions, it isn't going to change. More managers joined the conversation, and it quickly got very focused on technicalities within the particular problem, and the conversation drifted away from the theme of how they work together. I sensed an atmosphere of avoidance, which increasingly frustrated me, because we wouldn't get anywhere if we couldn't get closer to an inquiry into the embodied experience of participating in the conversations that led to these patterns. I was more and more doubtful that this would lead anywhere. My repeated attempts at inquiring into more emotional and relational aspects of the story didn't seem to lead to any openings.

After some drifting back and forth and a sense of confusion about where we were going, John, who had been silent for a while, said to Thomas: 'I've been thinking. You say, that at a certain point, you had doubts about some of the decisions. I wonder whether this is true. I think you knew pretty well what the consequences would be'. Thomas nodded and smiled in an insecure way – he was being recognised for his insight while at the same time being dressed down in public by his boss.

John continued: 'my question is, why did you allow yourself to doubt something, which you were actually quite certain about?' Thomas – looking embarrassed – said that it was probably something about choosing your fights in interactions with senior colleagues. At that stage, another senior manager Victor, in a resolute manner, jumped in. He said that putting all the responsibility on Thomas simply wasn't fair. Victor felt increasingly that his own mandate was up for negotiation with senior people in the other units. Animated – with a sense of anger underneath it – Victor said that it is very hard to take on his responsibility when his mandate is not respected by other people, particularly by the newly recruited senior executives being on the same hierarchical level as John. As a form of closing remark to his intervention, he sarcastically folded his body like an angry-looking gorilla, asking: 'have any of you tried to insist on your position and mandate in a conversation with Benjamin?' Benjamin was a newly recruited senior executive, who had already established a reputation of being hard to negotiate with. While Victor did his role play, the other managers laughed out loud in a cathartic way.

John looked perplexed. From conversations prior to the seminar, I knew that he was frustrated with the behaviour of some of his new colleagues. However, he was extremely loyal and would never criticise them behind their backs, which probably frustrated the managers. Forcing out some laughter, John pretended not to be offended, and said in his usual calm way: 'I am well aware that as a senior team, we are not always 100% percent aligned. What worries me is if you then automatically think that you can lean back and wait for us to align everything'. Victor, sensing the push back from his boss, said that he was always happy to go the extra mile, but it would indeed be helpful if their mandates were more respected in the rest of the organisation. There was still a bit of sarcasm there in the background.

There seemed to be a sense of recognition of the point made by Victor. I was beginning to feel that perhaps he had managed to express some of what more of them had been holding back: a sense of critique of the lack of agreement in the executive team, which created difficult conditions for all of them. Perhaps difficulties in the senior management team were played out through those reporting to them and perhaps inquiry into some of these experiences might help in understanding the pattern. For the first time at the seminar, it felt as if the exploration could create a new opening. I had something to explore further with John and with all of them.

Making sense of the narrative

Until this moment at the seminar, the group had seemed united within their powerless fragmentation. However, John's reflections on Thomas's story called out a strong response in Victor, a response which seemed to resonate with others. Victor took a risk in expressing a criticism towards the degree of disagreement in the senior management team. His response was implicitly a criticism of John's capacity to negotiate agreements with his colleagues in the senior executive team. At the moment where Victor made his point, despite the anxiety it evoked, the room suddenly felt refreshingly uncertain. How would John respond? What would emerge from this expression of difference made by Victor?

Interestingly, it was the very moment where Victor insisted on showing up as a 'who' that a potential for disrupting the stuck pattern finally emerged. My claim is that this 'showing up as a who' involves breaking through the administrative way of thinking and allowing himself to perceive John, Thomas and himself as human beings within a moral framework, where it was indeed possible to let each other down. There was a potential for a new beginning. The tiny exchange between Thomas, John and Victor seemed to shift something within the mood of the group. Others began speaking more openly about some of their frustrations in a way that didn't solely come down to questions about procedures and tools, but had more to do with interactions and interpretations of interaction. The problem wasn't solved, and whether the conversation would manifest itself as a shift in their way of engaging with each other would only be able to tell over time.

One of the generalisable qualities of the experience for me as a consultant is the struggle to overcome the superficiality of the kind of talk that manifested itself initially. This raises a question about whether the managers themselves thought that a focus on developing more nuanced procedures and process descriptions would solve their problem. From what happened between John, Thomas and Victor, I think it is clear that there was something else going on as well, something which is much more difficult to talk about due to the risk of the uncertainty of the response of the other. However, without finding ways of being together where people feel that it is worth the effort to speak up, how are the patterns going to shift? Without the possibility for the emergence of a public space for such conversation, where does such initiative for change mature?

Exactly this business about speaking up was central to Arendt in her work on plurality and political action. So what are her ideas on 'speaking up' and why is it important?

Plurality and the public realm

Arendt's interest in political action emerged as a response to her experience of the collapse of morality that happened during the Second World War. She was keen to develop a way of thinking about moral responsibility that could be an effective bulwark against the abuse of power that she had witnessed.

Having critiqued the Kantian notion of responsibility as following rules or doing one's duty, Arendt offered an alternative view. She argued that the question of responsibility has to be located in the activity of 'action', which requires thinking, rather than in the activity of 'work'. Within a paradigm of work, thinking is discouraged because of its inefficiency; 'work' is much more effective in the absence of thoughtfulness (Arendt, 1963).

By locating the question of responsibility in the activity of action, Arendt emphasised the importance of the condition of plurality: it is only through the experience of sharing a common world with others which we look at differently that it is possible to develop a shared and common sense (Arendt, 1958). Human individuals can join together and form a space amongst themselves, and in that space, different perspectives on the common world can be shared and discussed. Arendt calls this space 'the public realm', and this is a place for discourse and action. To Arendt, our reality discloses itself through our political action in the public realm, and therefore, political action is to speak and act in the public realm:

> The human sense of reality demands that men actualise the sheer passive givenness of their being, not in order to change it but in order to make articulate and call into full existence what otherwise they would have to suffer passively anyhow.
>
> (Arendt, 1958:208)

It is within this context of plurality that Arendt writes about the *dignity of politics*, which is linked to the possibility for debating important questions of the present moment, a kind of debate which allows a conversation to emerge, which involves thinking and judgement. Thus, for Arendt, politics arises *between* people, when they insist on speaking and acting in the public realm, taking responsibility for what is done in their name (ibid.).

A key characteristic of plurality is the fact that it is dynamic. The persons who inhabit the world are continually changing. It is within the dynamic quality of plurality that Arendt places her hope for the future: in natality, in new beginnings. So, inherent to acting politically is the potential for novelty, for new beginnings, for new initiatives (ibid.).

My curiosity about these ideas of Arendt in relation to the question of powerlessness and loss of freedom is related to the shift that I felt happened when, finally, Victor allowed himself to be provoked by John and to speak into the public realm. Arendt argues that it is through plural speaking and acting in the public realm that it is possible to develop a shared and common sense which resonate well with the experience. It was the act of expressing difference to the narrative of John's, and thereby drawing attention to the political rather than the administrative side of things that finally led to a constructive provocation which could allow for movement of that common sense.

Actualising plurality

There is a certain normativity in Arendt's writing when it comes to plurality and political action. Arendt developed her thinking on plurality and the public realm in thinking about the potential bulwark against the evils that she had witnessed. Arendt thus argued that plurality *should* be realised or actualised[1] (Loidolt, 2019). According to Arendt scholar Sophie Loidolt, there are two reasons for this normativity: the first is that acting politically through speaking and acting in the public realm is required if the world is to be kept from collapsing into monolithic frames where only a single voice gets heard (ibid.). This point is perhaps the most provocative in the context of management thinking, where critique and conflict are often marginalised in a rhetoric which promotes harmony, alignment and compliance (Clegg, 2006; Flyvbjerg, 2001; Willig, 2014). However, the potential for movement and novelty at the seminar began to happen as soon as someone (Victor) dared to challenge the singularity of John's voice.

The second reason is that it is through acting politically that it is possible for the individual to realise oneself as a person in plural interaction with others. For Arendt, even if speaking and acting involve struggle and conflict, being and becoming a self can happen only in this mode of being with others (Loidolt, 2019:152). It was within this being-with-others that Victor managed to take up his voice, and through doing that became a 'who'. And it is within this becoming a 'who' that the potential for overcoming powerlessness arises. In other words, for Arendt, the meaning and purpose of political action is human freedom (Arendt, 2005). In her perspective, freedom is not a state that can be earned once and for all but something that is realised by plural human beings only when they act politically together (ibid).

The human condition of plurality is actualised when people take the risk and speak and act in the public realm. As distinctive from being a 'producing we', this 'politically acting we' is a sense of community which arises in the togetherness and mutual dependence on others through activities of speaking, acting and judging (Loidolt, 2019:152).

Arendt was clear in stating that action is not a means to realising particular intentions or goals. Acting politically is an end in itself, and realised plurality is the greatest achievement of which human beings are capable (Arendt, 1958:207). However, the 'politically acting we' is a fragile field, which is:

> constantly challenged ... on the one hand, not to become petrified and close itself up in (a more or less suppressive) harmony; and on the other hand, not to disperse and dissolve the space of appearance.
>
> (Loidolt, 2019:229)

Working with these managers and struggling to get a conversation going where something could happen makes it evident just how fragile this 'we' can be. This public realm can increase a sense of vulnerability. At the same time though, it is also the publicness of the public realm that constitutes the possibility of freedom and natality.

Consultancy as political action

Throughout this chapter, I have been drawing on the work of Arendt to try to understand why senior managers working in large organisations can feel stuck and powerless in a context of wanting to improve their joint practices. I have made the argument that the dominance of instrumental rationality, which Arendt conceptualises through her concept of 'work' can marginalise the activity that she calls 'action', which is about acting politically through speaking, acting and judging in the public realm.

The second part of the narrative gave an account of my attempt as a consultant at creating such a public realm, where it is possible to actualise plurality through the engagement with a variety of perspectives and opinions. The narrative has given an example of just how difficult it can be to establish a sense of courage to show up as a 'who' – as a unique individual, but also how when that happens, it can create an opening for a different kind of conversation, within which it is possible to explore problems as they appear in the embodied experience of being caught up in interactions with others.

This line of argument raises questions about the practice of consultancy. What is the role of the consultant in this Arendtian view of actualised plurality?

In my experience, invitations to do consultancy work are often framed in the same instrumental rational language which I have critiqued throughout this chapter. Clients often express a need for certainty about what will happen and some sort of assurance that we will get to a predefined destination. This leaves me as a consultant with a dilemma about how I want to respond. How much of my scepticism about such a way of thinking about change am I prepared to reveal? Am I prepared to risk not getting the job due to presenting a view on change which is radically different from the one the client assumes?

In my experience, fixed answers to those questions don't exist. The answers are dependent on a variety of aspects which need to be taken into consideration. Following Arendt's normativity about actualising plurality, however, one point can be made: there is no refuge from responsibility for my actions through appeals to consultancy theories or models which replace the human capacity for thinking and judgement with rules and procedures.

This may sound obvious, but in practice, consultants are faced with a variety of situations where there is an ongoing expectation and pressure to comply with models, tools and techniques, and as such leave a sense of agency and responsibility with the model or the tool. At the seminar when Victor spoke up, I sensed a welcoming of a risk-taking, but I often experience the opposite: a pressure to limit the degree of uncertainty and instability that arise from open-ended inquiry. Whilst consultants are inherently constrained by participants in a process and as such strongly limited in their capacity to create change (Stacey & Mowles, 2016; Mowles, 2011, 2015), there are also moments where the response of the consultant can have powerful consequences in terms of whether a disruption of established patterns will happen. A crucial point in this context is that disruption of established patterns can't implicitly be equated to 'successful intervention'. Change isn't necessarily good, as it is impossible to predict the consequences. As such, consultancy is political action, and consultants have to live with the uncertainty of the consequence of their participation. The important point, however, is that there is no rising above these political processes (Mowles, 2011). This can be seen as a blessing or a curse. For

Arendt, it is first and foremost an agenda, and it is a practical activity of exercising thinking and judgement in the unique moment, something that needs to be practiced with courage, skill and restraint (Canovan, 1992:277).

Consultancy as attempting to create public realms for reflective inquiry

Thinking about consultancy through Arendt's concept of political action raises questions about the more concrete practices that this may involve. Key to political action is the possibility of speaking and acting in the public realm. In a context of consultancy, such a public realm can emerge when room for open-ended inquiry is created (Shaw, 2002). That is when the main ambition of a conversation isn't production of, for example, different scenarios or action plans, but rather a deepened sense of understanding, which can emerge from reflective inquiry into a plurality of experiences and voices.

Such inquiring processes can be destabilising and demanding and sometimes impossible to establish. Being socialised into thinking that being effective means producing something visible or tangible (flip charts, power points, forms), many people struggle to see a deepened understanding as a valid outcome of an inquiry process (Shaw, 2005). Another reason why such processes can be hard to sustain is the inevitable disruption of established power positions. An inquiry into a plurality of voices can easily manifest itself as conflicting perspectives competing to be heard and recognised (Mowles, 2011). In order for novel insights to crystallise, what is required is a joint capacity to tolerate and endure plurality, ambiguity and uncertainty. It is about preserving a sense of curiosity in relation to the opportunities that may emerge in the encountering of difference.

Richard Bernstein (2007) talks about such a practice as 'engaged fallibilistic plurality'. Fallibilism means that 'there is no belief or thesis – no matter how fundamental – that is not open to further interpretation and criticism' (Bernstein, 2007:327). Engaged fallibilistic plurality means:

> taking our own fallibility seriously – resolving that however much we are committed to our own styles of thinking, we are willing to listen to others without denying or suppressing the otherness of the other.
>
> (ibid:336)

This description may sound idealistic, and it does describe a form of experience that – just like the fragile 'we' – must be seen as a temporal and momentary achievement. However, for Arendt pursuing such a sense of 'we-ness' is not a luxury but a necessity if we want to experience meaning, reality and freedom. Only by engaging in political action in concert with others can a space of meaning open up and be sustained (Loidolt, 2019:244). It is through engaging in relevant activities with others that we can come to experience that 'freedom is a worldly reality, tangible in words, which can be heard, in deeds which can be seen, and in events which are talked about, remembered, and turned into stories' (Arendt, 1983:154).

Conclusion

In this chapter I have drawn on the insights of Arendt to argue that the sense of powerlessness and loss of freedom and meaning that one can experience as a senior manager working in a large corporation full of bureaucratic procedures and processes can be seen as arising from a tendency to think of management practice through the instrumental category of 'work', whereby the category of 'political action' is marginalised. The marginalising of 'political action' involves a lack of attention paid to relational, emotional and political aspects of everyday interaction. The 'producing we' that arises from this tendency involves a certain lack of relatedness, where the moral importance of the unique individual is neglected.

A response to this development of increased instrumentalisation in organisations can be found in the idea of 'actualised plurality', which entails the potential of momentary achievements of a 'we'. Then, it may be possible to experience a sense of freedom through being able to engage in a conversation where plural voices and opinions can get heard and become the starting point of debate. Actualising plurality involves speaking and acting in the public realm through which reality discloses itself as a manifestation of debate between the plurality of people involved. Such a conversation which involves a plurality of perspectives can lead to two important achievements: (1) the ongoing conversation about important decisions can be kept from collapsing into monolithic frames where only a single voice dominates; (2) through showing up in the public realm and engaging in relevant activities, it is possible for the individual to realise oneself as a person in plural interaction with other.

Thinking about organisational life through these ideas of Arendt raises interesting questions about the work of consultants. First of all, it must be acknowledged that consultants can't rise above the politics of an organisation. Consultancy is political action, whether the consultant thinks about it that way or not. As Arendt put it, there is no refuge from responsibility through an appeal to rules or slogans – or for consultants through tools and techniques. Consultancy is about exercising judgement in the midst of uncertainty. A key practice in consultancy however is attempting at creating and sustaining a public realm within which it is possible to engage with the plurality of views that emerge through exploration of a particular matter. Engaging productively in such conversations involves what Bernstein (2007) calls *engaged fallibilistic plurality*, where we – despite the certainty we feel about our convictions – keep the conversation open to further interpretation and criticism. Through this, it is possible to engage with a plurality of perspectives without suppressing or denying the otherness of the other. Through such engagement with difference is the possibility for the achievement of a 'politically acting we'. Such a 'we' is a fragile we and it is a momentary experience, but nevertheless it is important in order to sustain a sense of meaning and freedom.

Note

1 Arendt uses the phrase of 'realising' plurality, whereas Loidolt reinterprets that as 'actualising' plurality.

References

Arendt, H. (1958). *The Human Condition*. Chicago, IL: University of Chicago Press.
Arendt, H. (1963). *Eichmann in Jerusalem: A Report on the Banality of Evil*. London: Faber and Faber.
Arendt, H. (1973). *Origins of Totalitarianism*. New Edition with added prefaces. New York: Harcourt Brace Jovanovich.
Arendt, H. (1983). *Between Past and Future: Eight Exercises in Political Thought*. New York: Penguin.
Arendt, H. (2005). *The Promise of Politics*. New York: Schocken Books.
Bernstein, R.J. (2007). *The New Constellation*. Cambridge: Polity Press.

Brinkmann, S. (2017). *Stand Firm: Resisting the Self-Improvement Craze.* Cambridge: Polity Press.

Canovan, M. (1992). *Hannah Arendt: A Reinterpretation of her Political Thought.* Cambridge: Cambridge University Press.

Clegg, S. (2006). The Bounds of Rationality: Power/History/Imagination. *Critical Perspectives on Accounting.* 17, pp. 847–863.

Ehrenreich, B. (2010). *Bright-Sided: How Positive Thinking in Undermining America.* New York: Picador USA.

Flyvbjerg, B. (2001). *Making Social Science Matter: Why Social Inquiry Fails And How It Can Succeed Again.* Cambridge: Cambridge University Press.

Griffin, D. (2002). *The Emergence of Leadership: Linking Self-Organisation and Ethics.* London: Routledge.

Loidolt, S. (2019). *Phenomenology of Plurality: Hannah Arendt on Political Intersubjectivity.* London: Routledge.

Mowles, C. (2011). *Rethinking Management: Radical Insights from the Complexity Sciences.* Farnham: Gower Applied Research.

Mowles, C. (2015). *Managing in Uncertainty: Complexity and the Paradoxes of Everyday Organisational Life.* London: Routledge.

Rosa, H. (2016). *Resonance: A Sociology of Our Relationship to the World.* Cambridge: Polity Press.

Shaw, P. (2002). *Changing Conversations in Organisations: A Complexity Approach to Change.* Abingdon: Taylor & Francis Ltd.

Shaw, P. (2005). Conversational Inquiry as an Approach to Organisation Development: *Journal of Innovative Management.* 3, pp. 19–22.

Stacey, R.D. (2012). *Tools and Techniques of Leadership and Management— Meeting the Challenge of Complexity.* London: Routledge.

Stacey, R.D. and Mowles, C. (2016). *Strategic Management and Organizational Dynamics: The Challenge of Complexity.* New York: Pearson Education Limited.

Taylor, C. (1991). *The Malaise of Modernity:* Toronto: Anansi.

Townley, B. (2008). *Reason's Neglect: Rationality and Organising.* Oxford: Oxford University Press.

Willig, R. (2014). Emancipation: From Introvert to Extrovert Critique. *Advances in Applied Sociology.* 4(7), pp. 190–196.

5

COLLABORATION AS A POLITICS OF AFFECT

Robbert Masselink[1]

Introduction: The normalisation of collaboration

When people are collaborating with each other, they often do so in habitual ways. Many of them have become skilled collaborators in order to get what they want or desire. Ideologically speaking, a collaborative attitude reflects people's intentions to let co-operation prevail over competition by establishing a (temporary) coalition that raises the chance of attaining a common good unreachable when acting alone. This doesn't imply that collaboration isn't void of struggle or striving, but acting co-operatively implies constraining our actions with the promise of a future reward. This positions collaboration as a sensible strategy, a rational and reasonable consideration, to act and behave predictably in order to get what we want.

Co-operative behaviour strives for harmonious, conflict-free relationships and fits well within the concept of managerialism, the systematic approach used by managers to solve problems in standardised ways, grounded in the belief that organisations are more or less alike and that performance can be optimised by applying generic management models and skills. It is the application of performance management and audit-techniques, the use of surveillance technologies and the production of employees as proper working subjects that form the main aspects of managerialism (Costea et al., 2008). Together, they provide a governance structure that directs the conduct of people by means of techniques, discourses and programmes that mobilise people's capacities (Marshall, 2016). It isn't aimed at restricting and controlling people, as is often thought, but at making a particular kind of behaviour 'normal' (Betta, 2015) and accepted. Collaboration has become one such 'normalised' practice, making its ancillary behaviours appear legitimate, self-evident and habitual.

There is power in such habitual conduct. With collaboration having become firmly established within managerial practice, the legitimacy and identity of the people involved are safely secured. Collaborative conduct is based on the constant reiteration of past physical and verbal activities (Wright, 2017) and emphasises the functional character of their interactions in the light of a common good and a predictable relationship. It contains an affective component that reflects people's intentional feelings for others as the conjoint product of their historical interactions which triggers mutual expectations of each other every time they interact (Crossley, 2011). Feelings and emotions become patterned, predictable and recognisable, attuning people's bodies to the desired collaborative situation and attaching particular emotions and feelings to that situation (Burkitt, 2014). As a result, collaboration becomes a stabilising force by reifying people's interactions as predictable patterns bringing forth predictable outcomes.

The collusive potential of this stabilising force is the unconscious agreement among people to maintain the relationship, not to confront existing power relations and to avoid discomforting social emotions, such as shame and embarrassment (Curtis, 2018; Petriglieri & Wood, 2003). Collusion covers up the inherently uncertain nature of human relationships that people find difficult to talk about, reduces anxiety levels and releases the discomfort of an 'as-yet-unsettled' situation. Paradoxically, collaboration has become a habit or social strategy of including people's unique individualities within a conforming social practice that covers up the differences that exist between them. Part of this compliant behaviour is to treat each other in nice, friendly and collegial ways that will prevent others, and oneself, from becoming upset, anxious, competitive or hostile. In particular ways, this same pattern is going on within the consultant-client relationship.

Collaboration within the context of consulting

In popular literature on management and consulting, collaboration is described as a co-operative practice between a consultant and a client that, if enacted successfully by both, enables them to attain a common good. Within this practice, the consultant is considered to be a trusted adviser, even a coach, who provides knowledge, adds value (Marsh, 2009) and offers a solution for the problems, concerns and issues that the client is dealing with (Kipping & Engwall, 2002). Underlying the collaboration, they share a vision regarding the problem and the solution to be implemented, framing collaboration as a joint endeavour to resolve issues and implying a relationship of mutual dependence in which consultant and client need each other in order to succeed (Bushe & Marshak, 2015).

Collaboration fits well within the field of organisational development (OD) that contains an ideology of progress and improvement, which strongly appeals to managers and consultants alike. The consultant–client relationship is commonly characterised as a helping one (Coghlan, 2018; Schein, 1987), which allows for mutual inquiry and learning. The partnership that the consultant intends to attain positions the client as an active participant in the creation and dissemination of knowledge by means of dialogical conversations and meetings which they mutually produce, share and control (Cheung-Judge & Holbeche, 2011; Jones & Brazzel, 2006; Messervy, 2014). The collaboration departs from an agreed-upon common goal, outcome or objective (Weisbord, 1992; Shuman, 2006); there is an engaged attitude by all participants involved, a shared intention to bridge differences, enhanced openness of communication and information sharing and the development of mutual trust (Messervy, 2014; Schuman, 2006; Cheung-Judge & Holbeche, 2011).

This hasn't always been the case. Over the years, the consultant-client relationship has developed from an asymmetric into a more symmetric one. Originally, the client was considered to be dependent on the management knowledge the consultant provided him (Engwall & Kipping, 2013), alleviating the uncertainty that was, and still is, inherent in the managerial role (Sturdy et al., 2009). The consultant was considered to be the senior partner in the relationship (Fincham, 1999). In order to radiate the confidence and certainty that the client apparently needed, the consultant took control of the relationship by impressing the client and showing strong rhetorical skills (Clark & Salaman, 1998; Sturdy, 1997; Sturdy et al., 2009), hence establishing his reputation as an expert capable of reconstituting management control. A similar asymmetry can be detected in the psychoanalytic literature on consulting, where the consultant is supposed to be in control of the relationship with the client in order to reduce the uncertainties and anxieties that come from unconscious processes (Czander & Eisold, 2003).

This view of an active-passive consultant-client relationship has changed considerably over the years for several reasons. Scholars point to the fact that the consultant also faces considerable uncertainties because he has to establish his identity and a sense of control within his relationship with the client (Sturdy, 1997). Besides his expert role, the consultant fulfils a commercial one that is aimed at keeping the client, as a paying customer, satisfied and expanding the business. This double role enhances uncertainty (Alvesson & Sköldberg, 2009). As a customer, the client shook off his or her passive role and became an active and demanding participant within the relationship (ibid.). These factors shifted the power differential towards the client who became knowledgeable and acquired many of the skills and tools that were once the consultant's prerogative.

Functionalising the consultant–client relationship

Many managers have developed into consultant-managers, who now possess generic consulting skills themselves and have incorporated the consulting style into their management roles (Butler, 2010; Sturdy et al., 2015). Together with the difficulty of providing hard evidence for the effectiveness of consultants, the fragmentation of the consulting business and its changed labour relations, consultants face considerable uncertainties in their roles that impact the relationship with their clients. I believe that these trends reveal a paradox within the consultant-client relationship and probably in general for other professional relationships. While clients look for certainty and assurance within their relationship with the consultant, the consultant's dependency upon the client's participation turns the relationship into a complex, ambiguous and uncertain one. By excluding this complexity from the collaboration in order to provide a safe and predictable relationship, a facet of the nature of the collaboration is denied that will likely produce feelings of alienation, cautious behaviour and uncertainty towards each other.

Consultants have developed several strategies in order to cope with their paradoxical role. Some keep their distance from the client and position themselves as objective and neutral outsiders. They act as technical rationalists by claiming to be experts in particular fields, such as change management, and provide concrete solutions for objective problems. Hence, they mask or reject the political and the ethical dimensions of their work, leaving that part of the collaboration to the client (Sturdy, 1997; Alvesson et al., 2009). Other consultants have developed an opposite strategy by becoming 'helpers' or 'partners' to their clients, developing cordial and intimate relationships with them. In particular, consultants from the OD field have chosen such a processual strategy, rejecting an expert role and instead supporting the client in their processes of improving performance, learning, developing and sustaining growth (Hicks, 2010). Although they have become close to the client by partnering with him or her, the 'helping' consultant also rejects political and ethical dimensions of his or her work, taking a systemic view of organisations that ascribes a telos, or purpose, of its own to which parts of the system have to be aligned. This perspective removes daily politics from the scene by claiming that differences of interests can be reconciled through the company's common purpose and trying to get everybody 'on the bus' (Lambrechts et al., 2011). The ideology of an inclusive organisation is inherent in their systems perspective.

I believe that both strategies have become prevalent and normalised in many consulting practices. They reduce the complexity and ambiguity of consulting work by focusing on delivering functional solutions that help improve organisational effectiveness and reduce their own and their clients' uncertainties and anxieties. As a result of this change in power relations, the functional consultant has become skilled in managing the relationship with the client, knowing how to establish and maintain a collaborative relationship and to execute and manage improvement and change processes (Butler, 2010). He has become a specialist and a therapist, aimed at fixing what is broken or adding to what is currently missing. As supplier, he now must be proficient at maintaining a healthy, productive and sustainable relationship with the client. This has turned the consultant-client relationship into a new hegemonistic one in which the client, as the now powerful party, can allow himself to be more indifferent toward the relationship than the consultant, the less powerful one, can (Scott, 1990). What once was the consultant's prerogative, that is, of being critical towards the client, has become an undesirable aspect within the relationship and is banned from the collaborative relationship.

Although I have given a brief overview of the development of the consultant-client relationship over the years with regard to respective roles, attitudes and interaction dynamics (Engwall & Kipping, 2013), what actually happens within the interaction or collaborative process between a consultant and a client is still poorly understood (Sturdy et al., 2009). Little is known about the behavioural aspects of a collaboration between the two (Leung & White, 2006) and research from a micro-social perspective in scientific research is neglected (Van der Ploeg, 2010). In order to explain in more detail what consultants and clients are actually doing, I will next turn towards the daily practice of collaboration and introduce a case in which I facilitated a management conference for a client.

Case, first part: Chairing a conference

I chaired a two-day conference with a management team of a public sector organisation that is responsible for the provision of licences, surveillance and maintenance with regard to environmental issues. I was hired to help develop a new governance policy. This conference aimed at making decisions about its execution. The participants consisted of six senior managers, who together formed the senior management team: five out of 17 team managers; the internal strategy adviser; the secretary of the senior management team; and me. We had already known each other for a couple of years, as I had facilitated other conferences and off-site meetings with this group.

The morning programme of the first day had been productive but, for me, also rather long-winded. We had been exchanging opinions and viewpoints in a familiar, co-operative manner about topics on the agenda. I knew that some of the managers wanted to discuss a topical client case that consisted of considerable tensions among them. It had not been put on the agenda, but during my preparation with the secretary of the senior management team, we had agreed that I would propose at some point during the conference to spend time on it. So, right after the break of the first day, I introduced the client case, made my proposal and asked the group what they thought of it.

David, one of the senior managers, started talking first. His statement was clear: he didn't want to waste time on the issue and wanted to use the remaining time that day on the topic he had prepared. I asked what the others were thinking, and after a few seconds of silence (I sensed that people were clearly weighing what to say), some of them answered rather hesitantly, not as outspoken as David, that the issue should be skipped and the meeting should move on. It was Sue, the chief executive officer (CEO), who gave the final push when she said it was wise to go on to the next topic, although she didn't sound very convincing to me. No one spoke in favour of the client case, so we moved on to the next topic.

David had prepared that topic, which had resulted in a detailed document that the participants had received prior to the meeting. But instead of discussing the document as a proposal to be agreed upon, people started talking about its details, discussing clients, real-time cases and situations, about what had happened and what should be done. For the next hour, a cacophony of stories followed that for me as an outsider was completely incomprehensible. People didn't listen to each other, every story was countered with another story and another one and another one. Whenever I tried to bring the discussion back on track, somebody would interrupt me and add another story to the others. People were so focused on each other that I felt shut out from the interactions. They had literally turned their faces and bodies away from me and toward others. I noticed that I had physically moved to the periphery of the group.

People who sat silently, watching what was happening, started to look at me, signalling with their eyes to bring an end to it. I tried to interrupt the discussion once again but failed in this attempt as well. It seemed like there wasn't much I could do and I realised I had lost grip of the situation, which contributed to a growing feeling of anxiety. I noticed my self-esteem had taken a dive as well as my energy. I wondered what was going on. How could I regain control, especially because I saw that we only had a little time left before the day would come to an end. Suddenly, John, one of the senior managers, raised his voice and said it was time to end the day and go for a beer. With that statement he ended the discussion, and everybody fled from the table toward the terrace or left.

The embodied experience of interdependency

I had realised from the beginning that my proposal might light the fuse under the powder keg by introducing a sensitive topic. Despite my positive intention, I had involuntarily affected them in unpleasant and unexpected ways. Their expectations of a predictable, friendly and pleasant conference hadn't been met, mentally or emotionally. This had caused a disturbance and for some a breakdown in the collaborative contract we'd had up until that moment. It shows collaboration as a temporal phenomenon that is simultaneously affirmed and strived for while being denied and contested within people's continuous interactions.

The disturbance I caused didn't lead to a rational conversation of the pros and cons of my proposal. If it had been just that, then it wouldn't have been a significant moment, for me or others, in my collaboration with the client. The affect it had on others, such as David, was embodied. I had affected his and others' bodies in physical and mental ways that caused uneasiness, discomfort, anxiety and resistance. Stirring up unwanted feelings and emotions made them react in ways of wanting to restore the situation and 'get back to normal'. Emotions can be seen as disturbed habits and illustrate the collision between people's 'sense of self' and the social reality they find themselves in (Dewey, 1922/2007). Disturbed habit brings up fantasies of an unwanted future, which likely will result in attempts to restore control over the situation, their own bodies and maybe even those of others. Hence, collaboration regulates the behaviours, feelings and emotions of people by educating and socialising them in the customs of an established practice, which leads to particular kinds of knowing and thinking, and to feelings of belonging and authority that help create a 'we' identity (Elias, 1991). Everyone who deviates from what is considered normal and legitimate runs the risk of being corrected or expelled from the collaboration, which reveals underlying ideology and power relations.

People who want to collaborate with each other try to establish an unwritten contract upfront as narrative social coherence that contributes to relaxed bodies, harmonious interactions and predictable outcomes. But despite people's best intentions, such outcomes can't be guaranteed, as this case showed. Because when people interact with each other and become involved in discussions that matter to them, they evoke and provoke responses from each other that can't be controlled by any one individual. A rational-discursive concept of collaboration leaves out this embodied-affective dimension in which bodies resonate with each other in affective ways that reveal people's entanglements with each other, themes, personal histories and social-cultural backgrounds. As a result, purpose and a sense of mutual adjustment and recognition emerge from the constant processes of interaction among people, which are felt as embodied experiences.

Collaboration is enacted more than it is followed as a prescription, with the function of creating a joint sense of 'we', a purpose and a feeling of control and belonging that is experienced in embodied ways rather than conceptually. In reality, people affect each other continuously in voluntary and involuntary ways that, consciously or unconsciously, reveal people's interdependencies. Admitting the fundamental interdependence between people doesn't sit well with the ideology of managerialism that regards people as autonomous, independent individuals. Acknowledging people's interdependent nature brings differences, power relations and emotions to the fore. Removing this competitive aspect from the collaborative relationship and emphasising openness, equality and harmony serves to maintain current power relations and ideology.

Collaboration as the politics of affect

As an affective practice, collaboration emphasises a particular position, value or group identity and regulates people's interactions in a way that contributes to a joint sense of purpose and control. It includes people's identification on an affective level by allowing particular feelings and emotions that suit the collaborative relationship. Affective identification normalises people's interactions, giving them a particular shape that is experienced as joyous, friendly and amicable, which stimulates them to maintain the relationship. When interacting with each other, people 'feel their way forward' in order to maintain a particular form of relationship and a sense of relational coherence. Breaching these unwritten rules will likely result in negative judgement, exclusion, denigration or some other kind of judgement that can cause feelings of social shame. Collaboration implies refraining from opposing elements, such as competition, striving, contestation, conflict and difference, by means of self-restraint. It becomes a 'politics of affect' that tries to regulate people's behaviour and makes it appear normal to behave in harmonious, conflict-free ways.

However, in daily life, the embodied habitual dimension of collaboration will be reproduced, defended or challenged, as I did in the case I described, hence making collaboration simultaneously predictable and unpredictable. People not only co-operate but also compete with each other for topics to be discussed, outcomes to be attained and to be acknowledged for who they are, what they think and contribute. Consultants and clients alike can get a fuller understanding of collaboration when they accept and include these competitive aspects as well as the co-operative as an inherent part of it. Despite people's best intentions and efforts, others will often resist what they are trying to accomplish and push back at them (Brinkman, 2012). The resistance experienced creates an opportunity to reconsider one's relationship to the things that resist them, finding new knowledge and ways to cope with them in the future (Dewey, 1922/2007).

David resisted and rejected my proposal, pushed back at me, without considering my motives for doing so. His resistance was immediate and embodied with very little or no thinking about collaboration conceptually. He shattered the 'fantasy of distance' (Dale & Latham, 2014), which proposes that professionals act autonomously, are equal to one another, accountable for what they do, strive for a common purpose and complement each other's qualities and strengths. By contrast, he showed that he was involved personally and that something mattered to him, therefore he had tried to influence the situation and in which he succeeded. This illustration suggests that the collaborative relationship is an ongoing power-affect dynamic, mutually made and remade, with a predictable-unpredictable outcome, in which people are (sometimes deeply) involved. They are confronted with the otherness of other persons, which they can accept, deny or reject. By drawing boundaries, they position themselves as the same as well as different from others and as friends, adversaries or both at the same time. This ambiguous character of collaboration doesn't sit well with the conflict-free, harmonious image that establishes social and narrative coherence. Accepting otherness into the relationship implies including the agonistic or political aspect of collaboration by legitimising the identity, opinion and position of the other despite personal preferences (Mouffe, 2013).

Rejecting otherness might seem tempting, creating feelings of certainty, authority and predictability, but it comes with consequences. Without the acceptance of differences, people can't position themselves well against each other, collaboration as a process of joint sense-making doesn't happen and neither will a satisfactory collective identity develop in which people's individual identities are recognised and included. What is lost is the possible transformation of existing relationships, identities and priorities over time and therefore the chance for novelty and change to occur. Next, I will continue the case with my story about what happened the second day.

Case, second part: Reflecting on a confusing first day

When I entered the conference room the next morning, the secretary of the management team approached me and said that the discussion last night had continued on the terrace and become heated. The discussion among those who had stayed was about the case they had refused to talk about the previous day. I noticed other participants, standing in small groups, discussing what had happened on the terrace. Some of those arriving approached me to apologise for what had happened the previous day.

I opened the meeting, welcomed everybody and said that I wanted to reflect on what had happened the day before. I shared my experience of having felt myself becoming increasingly uncomfortable, not feeling listened to and ignored. Also that my attempts to regain control over the discussion hadn't been very successful. I wondered out loud if the team managers had had similar experiences with the senior managers in their daily work. I said I thought that the discussions we had had the previous day were papering over issues of real concern. Postponing them meant that nobody had to take full responsibility for them, but also that the decisions they were making during this conference might not lead to the changes they wanted and the organisation might need. The lack of a meaningful discussion now, at this conference, would likely contribute to insufficient commitment later on to the agreements that had to be made at the end of the conference.

I summed up what I thought were (some of) the issues that concerned them: loss of grip by teams on their workload, senior management interfering in operations, loss of integrity due to functional integration and applied pressure on teams to increase production. I turned towards the team managers to ask them if they recognised these issues. It was a deliberate gesture on my part, as I wanted to remind them of their expectations as previously expressed. I asked them if, by taking steps toward solutions for these issues today, it would make the conference valuable to them? I invited everybody to respond to my reflections. Then I stopped.

The group stayed quiet for a while. Sue, the CEO, was the first one to reply to my story:

> We're not afraid saying things to each other and find it difficult to let things pass, especially when the discussion, such as the one that we're having here, is important. Maybe that's why we find it so hard to reach consensus. But maybe it's not only about the content and also about the way we react to each other that makes a difference.

John replied to the last comment, saying that one thing they did was to start making critical remarks toward each other.

This raised another discussion about the difficulty the organisation seemed to have to finish things. As one of the team managers explained: 'We're very solutions-driven but never finish the last twenty percent of what we do. We're just not making it.' The discussion continued about the reasons for this behaviour, such as the lack of arguments for or against a decision being made, the lack of clarity about who would be responsible for it, the difficulty for managers to take charge of discussions and to complete them in a satisfactory way. A couple of comments were of a more personal and reflective nature. One team manager said: 'Well, it's easy, isn't it? I stay free and don't have to commit myself to anything.' Somebody replied: 'Yes, but you also lose something.'

Another team manager dropped the question: 'Why am I being asked to attend this conference? I don't know. Am I invited to collude with your decisions in order to validate them afterwards with the employees?' An uneasy silence followed. I held my breath, thinking and wondering about the content and nature of the invitation the team managers had received. Was it communicated as an instruction or an invitation? Had it been sent to them formally or casually mentioned by the senior managers? I didn't know because I hadn't been there, but I realised that it could explain their indifferent, remote attitude at the beginning of the conference. Sue replied his question by saying:

> No, Charley, that wasn't the reason. We've said to each other (the senior managers) that we don't see everything, and you guys see so much more about what is happening within the organisation that we need you in order to reach a decision. We've been selective and have looked carefully at the right amount of diversity at this table, being able to really test the decisions that we want to make. The consequence of it is that you become part of the decisions that we make here.

I noticed that Sue's answer satisfied Charley. I asked him if he wanted to add something. He said he was fine with it and thanked Sue for her reply.

The discussion slowly turned toward the topic of the conference. Then, somebody asked the group: 'So, are we going to commit ourselves, are we able to reach consensus here and do we contrast our arguments for and against the decisions we have to make?' The questions kept hanging in the air, and because of that and the time pressure, I suggested that the group come back to these questions at the end of the day. Then, I turned the group's attention to the agenda for the rest of the morning.

Reflecting upon personal experience

Sharing my personal experience of the meeting the previous day was an invitation to the rest of the group to share something of their experiences too. My outpouring was accompanied by ambivalent feelings about whether or not this was the right thing to do. Should I have shared my experience the way I had, which could be perceived by others as an analysis and judgement of the event, or just have asked the question about what had happened the other day and then become silent? Expressing ambivalence and ambiguity are feelings that don't sit well within a collaborative relationship permeated by managerialist discourse. From this perspective, collaboration is an amoral practice in which what is said and done is considered 'good' by and of itself, thereby abolishing the political and ethical from the scene. From an experiential point of view, however, collaboration is an aesthetic practice as well (Gherardi, 2017), in which people experience feelings and emotions that resonate with how they are affected by each other's actions and how this affirms or denies their identities, positions and chances within the group. Politics and ethics play an important role within collaboration.

The stories from the other participants expressed several concerns and desires about the group, such as how to reach for consensus, the experience of improper behaviour, not finishing up what they'd started and the lack of clarity about why people were invited. These are all relational issues that are circumvented, often in unconscious ways, by directing people's attention to the content of their interactions. It seems as if nothing needs to be discussed or changed with regard to relationships, roles, goals to be attained and power relations. But people affect and are affected by how they interact with each other, and often they have demands for a change in their relationship. However, the expression of their desire for such change is restrained by a well-designed agenda, current power differentials and other defensive behaviours such as hiring an external facilitator. Sharing personal experiences about what matters to people creates an opportunity to shatter this 'politics of affect' by turning it upside down and expressing the multitude of voices that exist, revealing the differences there are within a group despite intentions for collaborating or reaching common ground.

By expressing my experience of the previous day's events, I had positioned myself by drawing boundaries and making clear where I, as an individual, stood in relationship to the group and the event. The other participants' stories added new layers to mine. Their stories referred to discourses of collaboration, participation, of being diligent in one's relationships with each other and of mutual commitments towards each other. The reflections they shared revealed the consensual-conflictual nature of their negotiating discourses that were masked by the managerialist discourse of a collaborative effort aimed at taking joint action towards common goals. The different discourses that were simultaneously present challenged these actions and goals and competed with each other for dominance and attention. People's experiences of ambivalent feelings and emotions, such as mine in that instance, reflect the ambiguity of social situations they find themselves in. Negotiation is constant within people's interactions, and covering over this aspect, pretending that people are on the same page with their goals and agenda's while they're not, leads either to compliant, obedient behaviour or disengagement. When removing the agonistic aspect of collaboration from the scene, all that is left is a watered-down version of collaboration.

Collaboration as an affective ethics

Expressing personal feelings and emotions about the situation or event, as I did, creates an opportunity to consider that what people do, simultaneously enabling and constraining each other in their expressions and actions, affects their relationships and possibilities for future interactions. Proposing an affective ethics, set off against an actionable ethics, exemplifies a different view of collaboration: that of a performative process where people's action, what they do and say, has an effect upon others. As a consequence, the receiver(s) of people's actions will respond to it in conscious and unconscious ways that create an affect in the interactions. People's responses are pragmatic, in the sense that they will react in ways that keep their options for the future open. Hence, they actively participate in the situation they find themselves in, influencing it and being influenced by it at the same time.

This temporal perspective differs from a systemic one, in which people's interactions are aimed at reaching a common target while behaving in efficient ways to fulfil the system's purpose. But the goals of the conference weren't 'good' in themselves, nor shared by all participants. Their questions were not about goals and results but about the kind of relationships they found themselves in, about how to participate, what they were constituting together and what this meant for them as individuals, their sense of self, identity and position in the near future. Collaboration isn't solely aimed at externally set targets, but is an ongoing process of relational change and continuity in which people's future identities, positions and interests are secured and threatened at the same time.

Turning towards an 'affective ethics', the consultant can invite the client to reflect upon their collaborative relationship. When the client starts to express his personal experience of the relationship, positioning himself in relation to the consultant, the task and the situation, he introduces otherness into a relationship that is often highly functional. This allows for a more direct relationship in which the conversation can move to what is actually happening and how the situation is evolving. When the managers in the case started to express their experiences of the situation, they introduced difference into the conversation with nothing in particular that centred on the collective sense-making of the group. For consultants and clients, to work without an agreed-upon agenda or conversation topic is contentious terrain with little to hold on to. It can lead to surprises that can wreck the collaboration by exposing collusion or complicity. But enduring this lack of solid ground can also help a group to become unstuck from the patterns in their affective practice. I was able to endure this uncertainty for some time, but finally reached out for solid ground by directing the attention of the group to the well-planned agenda that had been abandoned.

I found it hard to stay in that place of uncertainty and ambiguity for very long, feeling vulnerable to the argument of whether or not this reflection led to anything worthwhile. Managers and consultants are, in a way, very much alike, in the sense that many of them act from the same managerialist discourse that prefers abstract, model-oriented conversations which give little consideration to subjective experiences of what is being discussed, hence making the concrete and tangible subservient to the rational and propositional. It is tempting for both of them to agree on abstract ideas that aim for a better future and more difficult to confront their differences in the actual interactions, leaving them outside the collaboration. Avoiding these differences contain the risk that consultants and managers are becoming deskilled in practising politics and criticising the sovereign 'good' of managerialist discourse. It affects their competences in practical judgement and collaborative skills, especially in taking a deviant position and inquiring into the different positions that others are taking or withholding from the relationship. Also, they may lose the ability to endure the uncomfortable feelings that come with the struggle and strive to understand each other's positions and arguments.

Conclusion

In this chapter, I have explored the experience of collaboration from a consultants' micro-perspective. This experience is different from the ideal descriptions of collaboration in the consultant-client relationship characterised by equality, mutual co-operation, openness and complementarity. Emphasising this ideal relationship between the consultant and client suits the managerial perspective of collaborating for a common purpose without unnecessary relational struggle if the parties involved stick to the rules of the collaborative game and restrain themselves in their behaviours. Such a perspective values the collective over the individual and will often result in a complicit or collusive relationship instead of a collaborative one.

The case, however, showed that a collaborative relationship between the consultant and the client doesn't favour the collective over the individual. Instead, it acknowledges that both are forming and formed by each other simultaneously. Collaboration emerges from the consultant's and the client's interactions and will affect those interactions in iterative ways. They are involved in the co-production of it, each affecting each other and dependent upon what they bring into the relationship with regard to personal histories, characters and preferences. Differences are constitutive of collaboration, bringing competition alongside co-operation. Consultants and clients co-operate with each other and compete; it is by the mutual recognition of each other's unique qualities and contributions and the willingness to accept the otherness of the other that collaboration comes about.

Rejecting the competitive or, what I call, agonistic element from the collaborative relationship means denying its political-ethical character. Collaboration isn't just a functional or instrumental endeavour to create value of some kind; as an ongoing process of shifting power relations, it is also an end in itself. Participants position themselves constantly in relation to each other, forming coalitions and oppositions, out of which meaning emerges that can be comprehended more fully when competition, conflict and struggle are accepted as inherent parts of collaboration. When these elements are avoided and contradiction and confrontation are no longer possible, mutual respect may decline and become antagonism. Difference then may take the form of a struggle between enemies (antagonism) instead of a struggle between adversaries (agonism) (Mouffe, 2013). The opposing perspective is judged as nonsensical, ridiculous or out of the question, emphasising the moral righteousness of the collaborator's own perspective.

I suggest an ethical perspective that allows for a plurality of discourses within the collaboration, hence accepting its agonistic nature. From this perspective, the consultant is always taking a position and no longer pursuing a neutral role or position. A sensible strategy is to leave this naive position behind and adopt an attitude of engaged disengagement (Trundle, 2018). He or she simultaneously participates in the collaborative relationship as fully as possible while keeping a reflexive attitude and being aware that others are judging the fulfilment of his or her role. Realising that he or she will always be partisan in the eyes of others can motivate the consultant to express thoughts and actions as clearly as possible. Marcus (2001) talks about collaboration as 'theatres of complicit reflexivity', which I believe is a good metaphor for the consultant to hold onto and stay aware of the 'positioning game' that he or she is always a part of. The disengaged aspect of this attitude allows for reflection upon what is going on and may lead to an invitation to have a collective, reflexive conversation, such as the one I had in the case discussed above.

Such a conversation will likely bring up irrational aspects that are considered undesirable or irrelevant from a managerialist perspective. Examples of such aspects are the responsibilities the consultant and client may experience for the relationship, each other and the consequences of their joint actions towards their immediate environment. These aspects emerge from their embodied relationship in which experiences of mutual affect, attunement, resonance or alienation (Rosa, 2020) can take precedence over its intent and output. Collaborating brings forth an affective knowing what is right and wrong and what is going on that will enable and constrain the freedom of the consultant and the client within their relationship. 'Knowing' how to act locally in a way that moves things forward emerges from the direct experiences that the consultant and the client have of each other, their relationship and the situation, which can never be designed or planned ahead.

Instead of assuming a smooth, co-operative relationship in which the consultant and client form a synergetic relationship, euphemistically called a partnership, they will affect each other in desirable and undesirable ways. In their responses towards each other, they will try to maintain their identities and future options or anticipate the likely consequences of each other's actions. This will inevitably result in surprises that, as my proposal in the case showed, can cause strong reactions when they are experienced as a breach of their (mostly unwritten) agreement. The consultant-client relationship doesn't exist in a vacuum, so surprises will occur in any case because of the actions of others and through unexpected events. Acknowledging the reality of being affected can run counter to seeing oneself as an independent and autonomous individual, admitting that the consultant and client are dependent upon each other for their identity, self-efficacy and freedom to act. When these are restrained, they can give cause to feelings of shame, embarrassment or anxiety, realising the risk of being socially excluded, ridiculed or denigrated. It reminds us that feelings and emotions serve a social function that makes people aware of the existence of power relations in what seems to be an open and equal relationship. They bring people's differences in values, norms and identities to the surface in situations where similarities are emphasised and 'we' is prioritised over 'I'. The social function of affect, what I call the 'politics of affect', is likely one of the reasons why we find it so difficult in business and other social situations to discuss our emotions and feelings. They reveal the inequalities that exist, the constrains that people put on each other's freedom to act and the self-restraint in people's behaviours that have become normalised aspects of our social interactions.

Individually or collectively experienced affect can illustrate moments of social breakdown in which people become unsure how to proceed. I described such a moment in the case when the discussion escalated and I felt myself excluded from it. Whenever a breakdown happens and the routine of collaboration is broken, accidentally or deliberately, an opportunity for reflection is created. Routine as a function creates certainty and predictability, hence a safe pattern of behaviour. Regarding yourself a strong collaborator, as a consultant, will likely lead to a preference to stick to your routine of facilitation or helping the client, keeping yourself and the client safe from surprises, uncertainties and insecurities.

Becoming aware of the 'politics of affect' creates an opportunity for the consultant to invite people to reflect upon their collaboration and to share their individual experiences of it. It offers them the opportunity to explore their differences, surfacing conflicts of interests, values and choices and creating an opportunity to reflect upon the political and ethical character of their collaboration as well as the repetitive patterns and group dynamics that they together recreate. Their reflections will likely bring multiple interpretations to the surface that reveal the differences that exist in a group and that are already part of the collaboration but not included in the conversations. An affective ethics can direct the attention of the participants towards these veiled experiences and towards the consequences of these cover ups. As a result, people may become disengaged from the collaboration, pretend that they're engaged while they're not, refrain from actively participating or become alienated from their feelings and emotions or sense of self. I suggest that when the consultant and client are willing to include the agonistic aspect of collaboration in the relationship, accepting that they are partners as well as adversaries, their experience of the relationship can become more realistic, complete and direct. Making their collaboration part of the everyday conversations and expressing personal experiences of it opens up the possibility of reflection that may increase the chance for a more open and direct relationship.

Note

1 This chapter presents work that was first explored in the author's 2019 doctoral thesis entitled "Collaboration as the Politics of Affect: The Client–Consultant Relationship as an Embodied Moral Practice" available at https://doi.org/10.18745/th.21803.

References

Alvesson, M., Kärreman, D., Sturdy, A. and Handley, K. (2009) Unpacking the client(s): Constructions, positions and client-consultant dynamics. *Scandinavian Journal of Management*, 25(3), 253–263.

Alvesson, M. and Sköldberg, K. (2009) *Reflexive Methodology: New Vistas for Qualitative Research.* 2nd ed. London: Sage Publications.

Betta, M. (2015) Foucault's Overlooked Organisation: Revisiting His Critical Works. *Culture, Theory and Critique,* 57(3), 251–273.

Brinkmann, S. (2012) *Qualitative Inquiry in Everyday Life: Working with Everyday Life Materials.* London: Sage Publications.

Burkitt, I. (2014) *Emotions and Social Relations.* London: Sage Publications.

Bushe, G. and Marshak, R. (2015) *Dialogic Organization Development.* San Francisco, CA: Berrett-Koehler.

Butler, N. (2010) 'Lessons for Managers and Consultants': A Reading of Edgar H. Scheins's Process Consultation. *The Leading Journal in the Field' Destabilizing: Authority in the Social Sciences of Management.* 61–84.

Cheung-Judge, M. and Holbeche, L. (2011) *Organizational Development, a Practitioner's Guide for OD and HR.* London: Kogan Page.

Clark, T. and Salaman, G. (1998) Telling Tales: Management Gurus' Narratives and the Construction of Managerial Identity. *Journal of Management Studies,* 35(2), 137–161.

Coghlan, D. (2018) Edgar Schein at 90: A Celebratory and Exploratory Metalogue. *Journal of Applied Behavioral Science,* 54(4), 385–398.

Costea, B., Crump, N. and Amiridis, K. (2008) Managerialism, the Therapeutic Habitus and the Self in Contemporary Organizing. *Human Relations,* 61(5), 661–685.

Crossley, N. (2011) *Towards Relational Sociology.* London: Routledge.

Curtis, G. (2018) *Functional Collusion in a UK Non-Governmental Organisation: Processes of Shame and Exclusion from the Perspective of an Organisational Development Practitioner.* (Unpublished dissertation, University of Hertfordshire, UK).

Czander, W. and Eisol, K. (2003) Psychoanalytic Perspectives on Organizational Consulting: Transference and Counter-Transference. *Human Relations,* 56(4), 475–490.

Dale, K. and Latham, Y. (2014) Ethics and Entangled Embodiment: Bodies-Materialities-Organization. *Organization,* 22(2), 166–182.

Dewey, J. (1922/2007) *Human Nature and Conduct: An Introduction to Social Psychology.* New York: Cosimo.

Elias, N. (1991) *The Society of Individuals.* Oxford: Blackwell.

Engwall, L. and Kipping, M. (2013) Management Consulting: Dynamics, Debates, and Directions. *International Journal of Strategic Communication,* 7(2), 84–98.

Fincham, R. (1999) The Consultant-Client Relationship: Critical Perspectives on the Management of Organizational Change. *Journal of Management Studies*, 36(3), 335–351.

Gherardi, S. (2017) One Turn ... and Now Another One: Do the Turn to Practice and the Turn to Affect Have Something in Common? *Management Learning*, 48(3), 1–14.

Hicks, J. (2010) *Co-Constructive Consulting: A Pragmatic, Relational Constructionist Approach*. Enschede: University of Twente.

Jones, B. B. and Brazzel, M. (2006) *The NTL Handbook of Organization Development and Change: Principles, Practices and Perspectives*. San Francisco, CA: Pfeiffer.

Kipping, M. and Engwall, L. (Eds) (2002) *Management Consulting: The Emergence and Dynamics of a Knowledge Industry*. Oxford: Oxford University Press.

Lambrechts, F., Bouwen, R., Grieten, S., Huybrechts, J.P. and Schein, E. H. (2011) Learning to Help Through Humble Inquiry and Implications for Management Research, Practice, and Education: An Interview with Edgar H. Schein. *Academy of Management, Learning & Education*, 10(1), 131–147.

Leung, K. and White, S. (2006) Exploring Dark Corners: An Agenda for Organizational Behavior Research in Alliance Contexts. In: Shenkar, O. & Reuer, J.J. (Eds), *Handbook of Strategic Alliances*. Los Angeles, CA: Sage publications.

Marcus, G. E. (2001) From Rapport Under Erasure to Theaters of Complicit Reflexivity. *Qualitative Inquiry*, 7, 519.

Marsh, S. (2009) *The Feminine in Management Consulting, Power, Emotion and Values in Consulting Interactions*. New York: Palgrave Macmillan.

Marshall, G. S. (2016) Neoliberalism and the Entrepreneurial Subject: Tracking Bevir's Decentered Theory of Governance. *International Journal of Organization Theory & Behavior*, 19(3), 361–371.

Messervy, A.S. (2014) *The Knowing Client: A Processual Perspective on Knowledge Shaping in Consulting Engagements*. (Unpublished dissertation, Business School, Queensland University of Technology, Australia.)

Mouffe, C. (2013) *Agonistics: Thinking the World Politically*. London: Verso.

Petriglieri, G. and Wood, J. D. (2003) The Invisible Revealed: Collusion as an Entry to the Group Unconscious. *Transactional Analysis Journal*, 33(4), 332–343. doi 10.1177/036215370303300408.

Rosa, H. (2020) *The Uncontrollability of the World*. Cambridge, UK: Polity Press.

Schein, E. H. (1987) *Process Consultation. Vol. 2: Lessons for Managers and Consultants*. Reading, MA: Addison-Wesley.

Scott, J. C. (1990) *Domination and the Arts of Resistance: Hidden Transcripts*. New Haven, CT: Yale University Press.

Shuman, S. (2006) *Creating a Culture of Collaboration, the International Association of Facilitators Handbook*. San Francisco, CA: Jossey-Bass.

Sturdy, A. (1997) The Consultancy Process: An Insecure Business. *Journal of Management Studies*, 34(3).

Sturdy, A., Clark, T., Fincham, R. and Handley, K. (2009) Between Innovation and Legitimation: Boundaries and Knowledge Flow in Management Consulting. *Organization*, 16(5), 627–653.

Sturdy, A., Wright, C. and Wylie, N. (2015) *Management as Consultancy: Neo-Bureaucracy and the Consultant Manager*. Cambridge: Cambridge University Press.

Trundle, C. (2018) Uncomfortable Collaborations: The Ethics of Complicity, Collusion, and Detachment in Ethnographic Fieldwork. *Collaborative Anthropologies*, 11(1), 89–110.

Van der Ploeg, M. (2010) *Samenwerken onder huwelijkse voorwaarden*. (Unpublished Master thesis, University of Utrecht.)

Weisbord, M. R. (1992) *Discovering Common Ground*. San Francisco, CA: Berrett-Koehler.

Wright, A. (2017) Embodied Organizational Routines: Explicating a Practice Understanding. *Journal of Management Inquiry*, 1–13.

6

SELLING OURSELVES SHORT

MARKETING THE SELF STRATEGICALLY: TOWARDS SUCCESS BEYOND RECOGNITION

Jacqueline Janssen[1]

Introduction

In this chapter I conduct a phenomenological and reflective exploration of how 'being on the receiving end' of a particular form of consultancy practice, career coaching, is experienced. I explore my own experience of being a part of the 'game' of career coaching and reflect on how my participation in this game influenced my sense of self. I found myself having to rely on a strategic branding of self to make my self more attractive to a degree that made me begin to question the connection with my experience and the identity that I co-created. In other words, career consulting services involve an invitation to a form of self-governing and performance, which can lead to a sense of alienation from oneself.

I suggest that the dynamics that I describe in this chapter have generalisable qualities to other forms of consultancy practice, since they rely on similar assumptions arising from managerialist processes. As such, throughout the chapter, I invite people who find themselves in consultancy roles to reflect upon the ways in which their texts, talk and practice invite others to perform and govern themselves.

The exploration is conducted from the perspective of 'complex responsive processes of human relating' (Stacey et al., 2000). Drawing on complexity sciences, this perspective on human organising is based on people being interdependent; 'radically' social and reasonable rather than autonomous and rational. Every person has expectations and intentions that influence the possibilities for interaction and the reaching of goals. It is the dynamic social interweaving of these multiple intentions which cause change and movement. Rather than focusing on the planning and prediction of outcomes, I suggest the significance of paying close attention to what emerges through these complex political webs of interaction. Reflecting on my experiences from the above perspective helped me to inquire further into how my sense of self was being constructed through coaching strategies which I found myself involved in.

The episodes which inform the narrative descriptions that I share below arose out of a situation of me seeking work some years back. I do still find, however, that those episodes have significance to me today, years later, as I work as a consultant in a different context from the one of career coaching. The significance is related to themes and questions arising in consultancy about the side effects of the dominance of a discourse, which invites us to conduct ourselves through strategic and abstract procedures where context may seem disregarded. When I use the term strategic coaching, I am referring to a thought style (Fleck, 1979) in which individual and organisational objectives are achieved through clear sequential steps often accompanied by visioning processes. Through this method, performance is claimed to increase, and targeted ideal futures are gained (Wilkinson, 2019; Fogde 2011). I will explore and critique this approach later. Through this, we can perform ourselves in ways that seem confident, but which at the same time covers over the messiness of everyday practice as well as the inherent uncertainty of identity.

BE-ing jobless: the struggle with sense of self

Finding myself immersed in a career coaching process, reading job ads, organisations' visions, missions and value statements in preparation for composing documents in accordance with strict prescriptions – strategically 'marketing me' – I experienced a sense of alienation from my self. I started to relate this to a rather confident and abstract way of speaking and writing about – what it is that we do in – organisations, leading to specific ways of describing what people in organisations (should) look like. My discomfort with such assumptions seemed to be shared by a significant number of jobseekers expressing the need to describe what was 'actually' going on; we seemed to identify more with a less abstract way of talking about ourselves and/in organisations than we were expected to in our career coaching trajectories. All of this prompted me to pose the question: In what ways could (strategic procedures around) career coaching be impacting our selves?

Doing doctoral research while at the same time being a jobseeker enrolled in a career coaching process highlighted three focus areas that seem to come together in producing experiences which left me feeling alienated and insecure about how to respond as a job seeker.

The first is the way in which career coaching processes are set up through a strategic management approach, which is underpinned by the ideology of *managerialism*. The second is *strategic management text and talk*; that is, the more concrete ways in which managerialism materialises in concrete situations between people. The third is the unavoidable component of *identity* in such processes.

In this chapter, I bring these three focus areas together to explore the experience of feeling under pressure as a jobseeker to manage my identity in accordance with strategic management text and talk under the influence of the assumptions inherent in managerialism. How do such experiences impact the ongoing formation of identity?

Recognition derived from work

I found that a lot of attention is paid to the impact of redundancy or job loss, not only on those forced to leave but also on those 'left behind' in, for example, scholarly articles, guidelines/trainings in organisations, outplacement trajectories and (professional) blog posts (e.g. Clark et al., 2001; Hareli & Tzafrir, 2006; Gandolfi, 2009).

My specific situation as a jobseeker and a researcher offered another opportunity: to explore what I experienced *after* the 'loss and mourning' period, my experiences in my career coaching process, described in the following narrative, which turned out not quite as smooth as it is often advertised or thought to be.

(Un)recognisable

Prologue

Moving from Thailand to be with my new partner in the French-speaking part of Switzerland, my life felt as though it was turned upside down. I had not cohabited for ten years; I became financially dependent because for the first time in my adult life I was not earning an income. I had no social network, did not speak the local language and the wintertime greyness seemed to close me off from the world. Although I felt appreciated by my partner, I felt insignificant.

When spring finally awakened, Switzerland began to appear more inviting, but the job market still seemed inaccessible. At a networking event, I talked to a few people; some advised me to hire a job coach as, in their opinion, doing things 'the Swiss way' was not easy to figure out by yourself.

I started defining my Professional Project, as my newly hired career coach called it, and at the same time was struggling in developing a doctoral thesis.

I worked around the shameful feeling of being unemployed; I networked, did voluntary work at a dual-career network for expat spouses[2] and took on a research project (with excellent networking opportunities) at a local university. I did not, however, find an official job.

At one point, I received an invitation from the dual career network to take part in a panel discussion at an upcoming event, so members could listen to our 'inspiring' stories. I responded that I was happy to partake and share my experiences but emphasised that I was still unemployed. The organising committee seemed not to mind.

Presentation

The event took place at a large multinational organisation. All seats in the huge room were occupied; people were standing along the walls.

Following the network's formal welcome, a human resources (HR) officer presented the host company. She described her organisation as being innovative and collaborative, cherishing values with which, she emphasised, employees engaged in a unique manner, as they would consider these in every decision taken. She also underlined the importance of diversity, stating that it was scientifically proven to increase an organisation's successfulness, hence theirs! It felt as though I was listening to a recital from a glossy brochure – the mission, vision and value statement of any large organisation.

After the introduction, members were invited to practise their job interview skills. In two workshop rounds, a corporate recruiter or a service provider[3] conducted mock interviews with volunteers, while the others could 'listen and learn'.

Recognition

The moderator had a difficult time quietening the buzzing conversations around the tables. From the stage, she announced the panel discussion with 'very special' guests, which included me. I noticed how this made me nervous. Would people be disappointed?

There were only three of us; I was in the middle. When asked to introduce ourselves, I felt a hot flush going through my body. The moment I was handed the microphone I started by confessing that I was on the panel 'illegally' as I had not found a job. To my relief, laughter rose from the audience. My tension subsided.

I found myself replying to the questions posed very much from 'within' my own experience, not in a prescriptive and overly confident manner, as my fellow panel members seemed to do. I felt compelled to relate my personal take on what I perceived to be our shared experience, at times anxiety-provoking and disturbing. Afterwards, standing around the luscious buffet lunch, I barely had a chance to eat, as several people approached me to say how much they appreciated the way I had put into words what they were going through. They felt understood, recognised by and recognised themselves in what I had said – describing our shared experience of ambivalence and anxiety. This made me feel recognised in return. It felt good.

Outside-in

Despite being jobless, the career coaching process somehow increased my sense of connection to organisational life. I was constantly occupied by organisational matters, as collectively we (myself, coaches, fellow jobseekers, authors of articles/blogs, etc.) stressed the necessity to explore 'the market', define 'target' employers, tailor documents to match specific requirements, engage in networking, establish contacts and so on. Yet, being involved was no match for being inside, of which I was constantly reminded at career events and in 'How To's'.

The disturbances and anxiety I experienced in my job hunt, as had other jobseekers I spoke with, seemed not to be generally acknowledged, judging from audience responses to the panel discussion described earlier. Among other jobseekers, talking more freely, I gained more insights into management issues than I ever had when working. It was like the 'coffee machine conversations' in organisational life. We did, however, exercise caution in what we shared, given that at any moment one of us might get hired and become a valuable connection in our struggle to 'get back in' or we might suddenly find ourselves in competition. We needed to overcome our anxieties, sustain confidence and get on with the next application or, when successful, become fully immersed in the new workplace, 'staying in' and forgetting about our struggle.

As a consultant I notice similarities: I am expected to know the market, keep close contact, share stories, successes, like and support, recommend media such as LinkedIn and tailor my proposition to the current trends in my area of expertise, using words that are current and uttering my anxieties in informal settings with the same caution as described above.

Involvement and detachment

The process I went through appears to bear resemblance to what the German sociologist Norbert Elias describes in his paper 'Problems of Involvement and Detachment' (1956). Elias outlines how deep involvement (irrational, subjective) (ibid., p. 226) in matters over which we have little control can block our ability to form more 'detached' (rational, objective) concepts of these matters, limiting our horizon. Elias argues that this embodied involvement has shifted over time through 'processes of social change' (ibid., p. 231), where we become interdependent with increasingly larger numbers of people. Since we rely on a growing number of people, it is therefore increasingly unpredictable how our actions will be taken up by others. Therefore, over the course of what he terms the civilising process, we have developed the ability to execute impulse control, to take a 'cooler' and more detached position and to restrain ourselves from responding immediately from within the heat of our involvement. As a jobseeker, I anticipated that career coaching would help me gain a position of detachment. However, this appeared to be not entirely the case – at least, not in the way I was anticipating. In career coaching, just like in other forms of consulting, tools and techniques are often used in ways which prevent us from getting stuck in the messiness of underlying anxieties, interests and relations of power. As such, they provide a degree of detachment from the heat of our involvement. What I came to experience quite profoundly, however, is that this form of detachment functions in a way of covering over this mess.

As such, being enrolled in career coaching allowed me to experience one form of detachment, which stood in stark contrast to the form of detachment I experienced as a researcher relying on a method of 'taking experience seriously'. This research method requires me to face myself as an immediate participant from within (ibid., p. 234) and to detach myself from my experience in order to widen my view and enable myself to discern the changing configuration of the patterns I was forming with the people throughout my 'web of interdependence' (ibid.). To reflect, think and be reflexive, to think about my thinking; and all of this *in the moment*, experiencing – paradoxically – involvement and detachment at the same time.

These are two very different forms of detachment, which – as I'll come to argue – have very different implications on identity formation.

The metaphor of the game

So there I was, caught up in career coaching in a way that made me feel alienated, trying to make sense of the experience, trying to become detached about the involvement. Here, Elias's concept of 'the game' proved helpful as a way to 'examine questions of power without being emotionally involved' (Elias, 1978, p. 93). Looking at career coaching as a strategic game, learning to identify the 'players', inquiring into their intentions, preconceptions, goals and finding out that 'who is more or less dependent on the other ... has to adapt himself more to the other's demands?' (ibid., p. 79). It proved useful to consider the differentials of power between all players, including myself, rather than focusing solely on myself, to take account of the entire group of players or of the game 'itself' (if indeed such a thing is possible). In my consulting practice, this perspective lessens my emotional involvement to a degree, not necessarily making me a 'better' player, but certainly helping me to be more aware of stakes and interests, of assessing risks, influencing the game, perhaps even contributing to the constitution of another game.

I am not trying to define the game, spell out its rules for other consultants to be able to follow my instructions and get better at it – in other words, reifying the game as an object as if there is only *one* definable game. Rather I argue that the metaphor of 'the game' can allow consultants to immerse in organisational 'games' *while* letting themselves be guided by 'practical reasoning' (Bourdieu, 2003): being in the moment, interacting with people, enabling themselves to notice what emerges, instead of pursuing set goals in a fairly mechanistic, prescribed manner.

With hindsight, I believe I developed a feel for the 'game' throughout my working life, as most professionals do, but the experience of being enrolled in career coaching made me doubt my expertise once I found myself 'outside' and inhibited by the strict prescriptions of strategic career coaching, further explored below.

Career coaching

Nowadays, it seems a pervasive belief that we need to become lifelong learners in order to enter organisations and remain employable, as constant change is accepted as inevitable:

> Key competences for lifelong learning [...] the ability to search for the education and training opportunities and guidance and/or support available is essential for an individual's personal fulfilment, professional development and social integration.
>
> (Council of the European Union, 2008, p. 2)

This notion leads to widespread efforts to prepare, coach and mentor people so they are ready for this arduous task from as early on as possible:

> As researchers emphasize, career related learning in the elementary school should 'focus on students' awareness of educational, occupational and other choices ... of ways to anticipate and plan for them ...'.
>
> (Herr et al., 2003, p. 334 in Sidiropoulou-Dimakakou et al., 2013, p. 23)

The emphasis on planning or strategically managing your career from primary education onwards points to an exceptionally strong conviction of its importance. Even when education has been completed or the next career step is to be taken, the need for assistance in managing careers continues to be underlined:

> It's no secret that it's still a pretty tough job market out there ... Fortunately, there are a growing number of professionals out there who can help make your search a bit easier – people like Donna Sweidan: The goal is to support people in making informed decisions about their career development and trajectory, as well as to offer various tools that they can use to meet those goals such as a solution-oriented approach, which involves working with clients to see what concrete steps they can take to achieve career objectives.
> (Cheek (for LearnVest-Forbes), 2013)

The 'tough market' can be entered successfully with support from the career coach, who can help define our goals and provide advice in the form of concrete steps to achieve these[4] (strategic management approach), but only if we follow up on the advice we are given:

> If clients are no longer doing the work required ... the utility of career coaching will decrease. I have a client who's currently in this situation. He knows what he wants to do, but for some reason, he's sabotaging the process by not heeding my advice to revamp his resume and network effectively.
> (Cheek (for LearnVest-Forbes), 2013)

Sweidan stresses that it is a widespread misconception that career coaches actually find people a job. Nevertheless, she seems to believe that the methods and advice she offers will probably get us where we want to be: 'doing the work required' (prescribed) is the right way to achieve the goal. Furthermore, 'not heeding advice' is considered 'sabotage', pointing to the huge importance that coaching is thought to have in achieving desired goals.

There are several assumptions in this that are worth questioning: that there is *a right way* of going about the job hunt; that a client 'knowing what he wants to do' means that his *aim is crystal clear* and will lead to him making *rational decisions* in order to reach this goal; that follow up and networking will bring about the *preferred outcome*. Building on Elias (1956), what seems to be overlooked here is the embodied involvement of the client, which may impact him and his 'clear view' of what he wants; also, little attention is paid to the highly social process of following up and networking, in which power relations largely dictate what connections can or cannot be made.

In the social contexts that consultants become part of, where one is interdependent with many people (possible clients, contacts, competitors), they have most probably experienced that it is unlikely that there is *a* right way leading to success. The same goes for the processes consultants use working with clients, for example, a director of a company often has a clear idea of what is required to be achieved. Consultants will work to achieve consensus on set goals, yet still there are many obstacles to be found along the way leading to different outcomes, which may vary from perfectly suitable (in hindsight) to unacceptable. Not working rigidly towards set goals may be a cause for conflict with the client; however, in my experience people know – often even acknowledge and/or accept – that it is never a smooth ride and outcomes are always uncertain to some degree.

Governing

Although career coaching and methods and tools related to this have been researched extensively, often with positive outcomes and/or recommendations for improvement, the process has also been the subject of critique. A number of researchers regard career coaching to be (self-)governing or coercive, 'a disciplining process at work' (Darmon & Perez, 2010), which may 'encourage commitment' (Krejsler, 2007, p. 473) but could just as well 'be turned into manipulative power instruments, or be reduced to shallow rituals' (ibid.).

Fogde's 'fieldwork and participant observation of career coaching'[5] (2011, p. 68) underlines that 'practices of writing a CV and preparing for job interviews' are generally understood as 'an instrumental project which is to be managed and achieved' (ibid., p. 79); but she views such practices more as 'a multifaceted process characterized by tensions' (ibid., p. 78). In her article, 'Governing Through Career Coaching: Negotiations of Self-Marketing', she mentions Rose's 'governing through freedom' (Rose, 1999). Furthermore, Rose describes how governance has changed over time, from being imposed on people by measures from 'the government' to contemporary government operating 'through the delicate and minute infiltration of the ambition of regulation into the very interior of our existence and expertise as subjects' (ibid., p. 11). Rose argues that people have come to see themselves as subjects who can close the gap between who they are and who they could or should be with the help of 'experts in the management of the self' (ibid., p. 11), who believe they are free to choose their way of life and who are to some extent unaware of the (self-)regulating forces brought about by 'normative judgement':

> Rather than being tied rigidly into publicly espoused forms of conduct, a range of ... 'lifestyles' are on offer, bounded by law only at the margins. Forms of conduct are governed through a personal labour to assemble a way of life.
>
> (ibid, p. 230)

In the 'assembly' of this 'chosen' lifestyle, career choice plays an important part. To be successful in pursuit of their chosen goal, a person should (govern themselves to) 'incorporate a set of values from among the alternative moral codes disseminated in the world of signs and images' (ibid., p. 231). In this context, as already discussed, career coaches are viewed as experts who can help to acquire the necessary moral codes and dexterity with the appropriate signs and images, managing us towards the strategically constructed, sellable selves which match the desired career. Once the 'free' choice to engage with the expert is made, the subject starts playing the 'career game'. This notion of game is well described by Bourdieu and Wacquant:

> We have an investment in the game, *illusio* ... players are taken in by the game, they oppose one another, sometimes with ferocity, only to the extent that they concur in their belief (doxa) in the game and its stakes; they grant these a recognition that escapes questioning. Players agree, by the mere fact of playing, and not by way of a 'contract', that the game is worth playing.
>
> (Bourdieu & Wacquant, 1992, p. 98)

As career coaching is broadly 'advertised' as the ultimate 'tool' to teach us how to play the 'career game', it is difficult to reject and attractive to engage with, especially for those lacking in self-confidence. Once 'in', Bourdieu and Wacquant suggest, we cannot question the rules if we want to succeed and we acknowledge the value of the game the moment we 'choose' to become a player, a 'choice' achieved virtually unnoticeably through self-governing.

In this context, it is conceivably difficult to be critical about our 'self-chosen' engagement, the expert status of the coach (consultant) and the given rules. Following procedures without question often means conforming against one's own judgement. This can happen for a variety of reasons plausible to the person. Being invested in the game, in my experience, dampened my urge to critique procedures and led to merely questioning *how* to use them, as in Fogde's observation:

> The students do not openly resist in the sense of questioning self-marketing [the procedure] but they negotiate and show ambivalence towards *how* to market the self.
>
> (Fogde, 2011, p. 79; emphasis in original)

Thus, the following appears essential: in the name of efficiency, uniformity, certainty, we seem to have become accustomed to using strategic management tools and techniques towards set goals. Generally, we do not openly question these procedures and their outcomes (probably sensing we may be taking a risk if we do). Rather, we may start to distrust our abilities, our 'practical reasoning' (to borrow Bourdieu's terminology). Some of us may even be unable to discern why we feel uneasy with the procedure and/or its outcomes. These signals of uneasiness, both from clients and experienced by consultant themselves, need to be addressed, as these may draw attention to what we are losing sight of. Focusing too much on the (successful, well marketed, simple x-step) procedure may distract us from what it is we try to meaningfully achieve together as well as from how this focus impacts our sense of self. Hence the focus is again upon the individual in isolation rather than the means by which individualities are continually being relationally constructed.

Good advice

Fogde (2011, p. 76) notes that the 'experts' provide 'general advice' to 'guide the subject in certain directions, but when it is negotiated with students it is often stressed that employers are individuals with subjective perspectives and there are no "rights or wrongs"' (ibid., p. 75). This seems to be related to Bourdieu pointing to the game following 'not explicit' and 'codified' 'regularities' (1992, p. 98) rather than rules, suggesting a provisional character and underlining the need for particularisation of general rules to suit the specific situation – something that is given scant attention, for example, in popular 'How To' guides.

What is both interesting and potentially disturbing here is, on the one hand, encountering a coach who confidently portrays curriculum vitae (CV) preparation as a trustworthy aid producing reliable outcomes, and on the other, finding this negated by experience.

I can understand that superficial impressions of 'certainty' might encourage the jobseeker as well as clients, staff and personnel we work with as consultants, and make them feel more at ease, secure and in control. However, for people who are anxious at the outset, first being convinced that the (often costly) coaching procedure – consulting process – will help them to be successful, then being confronted with continuing uncertainty despite the efforts of someone whom they regard an expert may intensify their anxiety. Indeed, the cause of their unease may be less easy to define, and perhaps even more difficult to overcome, given that people in demanding circumstances often blame themselves for negative results and feelings of inferiority towards the seemingly self-confident expert.[6]

Owing to the fact that I was researching my experience of being enrolled in career coaching, I increasingly became aware of the games that I got caught up in. However, I was taken by surprise by the great impact this game could have on me. It had not dawned on me that allowing myself to get invested in this game would also lead to a form of self-governing, which made it hard to become reflective about my experience. The experience added greatly to my understanding of the seductive nature of such enticing perspectives. As a jobseeker, I did get clues that something was wrong. I became anxious, started to distrust my own judgement and even went against it.

When I sense something like this happening in my consulting practice today, I attempt to 'return' to the 'researcher perspective' as described earlier, reflect on (the possible impact of) my 'expert role' and invite the person or group to explore the situation we find ourselves in.

Strategic management text and talk

As well as the issues in the procedures described above, I perceived the pressure to use 'appropriate' language, to 'present and improve ourselves', to be policing, controlling and labelling (Orwell, 1987). We jobseekers were moulded – but at the same time were moulding ourselves and each other – into an image that we hoped would be attractive to potential employers. In a sense it was attractive to us, too: it seemed to boost our self-confidence.

Sticking to 'general'/abstract terms may feel safer, depending on your interdependence in the relations you find yourself in (Elias, 2001, p. 52). We must estimate the risk of opening up, making matters more concrete, particularising the general, which inevitably means becoming more vulnerable, not being in control. At the panel discussion, recounted in the narrative, I found myself talking 'differently' and only afterwards realised that I had taken a risk by not speaking 'appropriately'. I could have undermined the work and status of career coaches in the room, the shared belief in their ability to release a person's potential:

> [A certain method] consists of powerful, proven coaching techniques and strategies that can define and release your infinite career and business potential.
> (The National Black MBA Association, 2014)

Conversational patterns

I deliberately choose not to use the term 'd/Discourse' here, as this has been used in a variety of ways (Alvesson & Karreman, 2000). In this context, I prefer 'language use' or (managerialist) 'conversational patterns' drawing on Shaw (2002), as this underlines that I do not refer to *one* clearly discernible discourse. Rather, I discuss patterns that show certain similarities.

Although language is discussed in articles around career coaching, these usually focus on *discursive practices*, negotiated talk in the construction of a 'sellable self' (e.g. Cremin, 2009). The impact of patterns of language used, the wording, seems to be less explored, which I look into in the following.

Paradoxical patterns

To support the notion of a stable, controlled environment, the use of language in strategically managed organisations needs to be as rational and unambiguous as possible.

The language I encountered in the course of my job search (e.g. in vision/mission statements) nonetheless seemed paradoxical: in many ways, it appeared to confidently describe a straightforward situation of complete control (efficiency, performance, planning, measurability), yet it could also be described as 'euphemistic' and 'provisional' (Jackall, 2010, p. 144).[7] Moreover, it appeared highly subject to management trends/fads (Abrahamson, 1996), identifiable by the frequent use of (new) 'buzzwords' (Spicer, 2013, p. 658).

How did the managerialist language seem to become enmeshed with this 'trendy' (Spicer, 2013) and 'euphemistic', 'provisional' (Jackall, 2010, p. 144) text and talk?

The most fundamental change, I believe, has been brought about by what Elias has termed the 'longer chains of interdependency'[8] (2000), the influence of countless human actions in a complex chain that can link many separate, multidivisional and/or hierarchically layered organisations nowadays, which make control and planning increasingly problematic.

In such complex environments, being too clear, direct or certain in one's statements (e.g. about percentage of efficiency improvement) may cause unwanted situations (e.g. failure, loss of face/credibility) over time. According to Elias and Rose, this risk leads to increased self-restraint. And as Jackall notes, this goes together with certain preferred language patterns:

> Most often when managers use euphemistic language with each other [...] the implicit understanding [is] that should the context change, a new, more appropriate meaning can be attached to the language already used.
>
> (Jackall, 2010, p. 144)

Giving ourselves some 'leeway' in this manner, Jackall underlines, is not intended to deceive:

> Managers past a certain point ... are assumed to be 'maze-bright'[9] and able to 'read between the lines' ... and to distinguish accurately suggestions from directives, inquiries from investigations, and bluffs from threats.
>
> (ibid.)

Certain conversational patterns in job ads could be a front, a filter – a firewall, if you like – to select those who are best equipped (or dare) to bypass official paths: networkers, people with contacts, people knowing how to play 'the game of games'[10] (Mowles, 2015, p. 108). Experienced players' strong 'feel for the game' (Bourdieu, 2003, p. 25) will probably alert them to the possibility of using different strategies. They may feel no need to follow the 'simple rules' commonly dispensed to less experienced (and less confident) players.

This language pattern seems to be well suited to portraying oneself – and the organisation in which one works, or would like to work – with confidence. In a euphemistic manner, it is possible to lay claim to various trendy skills and competences (e.g. 'sensitivity', 'intra-institutional action', 'fostering integration') that enable one to plan, measure and control one's work and steer the organisation and oneself in the right direction, towards desired, preferably common, goals. It conveys a sense of confidence and control, and where these are weak or even lacking, euphemisms and provisional wording can camouflage this. While this allows some leeway in describing positions, tasks and organisations, which can be useful when dealing with uncertainty, its ambiguity can also be problematic, as the candidate relies on the job description for crucial information, in a similar manner as the consultant does on the client briefing.

Strategic language use

Struggling to put my finger on what worked in the texts and what didn't, I realised that the most helpful information lacking in the job descriptions was something that could not easily be contained in words: *socio-political context*, which is often largely left out of consulting briefings as well.

In many cases, certain traits were attributed (solely) to the candidate. Yet I have come to understand from experience and research that the tasks described in these job descriptions are only possible in, and because of, the socio-political environment: our interdependencies and interrelatedness with other people. In our radically social context, where people have varying interests and intentions, sentences such as those listed below seem problematic (taken from several vacancies posted online on Intermediair (2014):

- Deliver profitable growth of the business in line with sales targets
- Maintain high-level contacts and relationships with customers
- Proactively create opportunities
- You can form independent opinions

These activities or skills are all socially enabled and restrained. An example to explore further:

> You take sufficient account of the interests, positions and responsibilities of aaa, bbb and ccc and create an open environment where all stakeholders feel valued and motivated.

Can one take *sufficient* (how much is that, and for whom?) account of all interests (how do we acquire this 'information' which is not always 'available'?) and create an open (what does 'open' mean to whom, and how much openness would be 'appropriate'?) environment (on one's own), where all stakeholders feel valued and motivated (idealisation)?

Although I find this example abstract and highly idealised, it does to some extent indicate the environment in which the candidate may participate; it describes, however briefly, the social network and interdependencies that underlie such major tasks. Nevertheless, it would appear difficult to express these complex situations in more meaningful words, to paint a more 'realistic' picture, if this is ever possible (or indeed desirable!).

Every person is formed by and at the same time forms society, which consists of the groups to which one belongs. To develop our understanding of our groups, we form a sense of the 'generalised other' (Mead, 1992, p. 154) that allows us to interact with people in ways appropriate to that particular group. We use 'common' language – significant symbols that call out the same response in ourselves as in other members of our group (ibid., p. 71) – and adhere to group norms and values.

It seems that the co-creation of meaning through social interaction is what is difficult to replicate in these prescribed, abstract ways of writing and talking about ourselves and organisations in procedures, to the point that they may seem only vaguely related to actual experience. People may feel disconnected from their selves, from their group (organisation), as they cannot recognise themselves in or relate to the text and talk they encounter or produce themselves.

Fashionable patterns

It seems important for higher circles of management to appear 'up-to-date' on 'the latest trends in managerial know-how' and not 'appear stodgy before one's peers' (Jackall, 2010, p. 149). These management circles fuel 'the industry of consultants and other managerial sages' (ibid., p. 150). Abrahamson refers to these as 'fashion setters', whose aim is to keep ahead of the competition, leading 'the forefront of management progress' (1996, p. 254). In this ongoing process, it cannot easily be determined who is driving whom, management or fashion setter.

According to Birnbaum, fashion setters stating the new technique (fad) they bring is:

> [...] both necessary and sufficient to transform the organizational sector; true believers may present their views with messianic zeal and suggest that the success, perhaps even the survival, of the sector depends on adopting this innovation.
>
> (Birnbaum, 2000, p. 6)

These fads tend to bring with them new or rediscovered buzzwords. The difficulty in challenging buzzwords lies partly in the fact that they are often not easy to 'resist': who would not want to 'show respect', to 'support sustainability'? When the novelty wears off or the word becomes devalued through overuse, new terminology is soon introduced (Spicer, 2013).

Just words

My experience being enrolled in career coaching suggests that we seem to have a tendency to take our responsibility for our actions more seriously than our words. Understanding text and talk as action may increase our awareness of the impact of language and encourage us to pay closer attention to what we say and write as well as what we do. Mead's social behaviourist understanding of language, of words, as acts provides an important view:

> There is a great range in our use of language; but whatever phase of this range is used is a part of a social process, and it is always that part by means of which we affect ourselves as we affect others and mediate the social situation through this understanding of what we are saying.
>
> (Mead, 1992, p. 75)

For Mead, meaning emerges in an ongoing social process of gesture and response, mediating the social situation and affecting all those involved; all words (gestures) are (phases in) social acts, language is action. Of major importance in this is 'mediating reality', which suggests that words are used as a medium to describe, to make sense of reality as we (want to[11]) perceive it. Then, in what ways can a paradoxical conversational pattern, both 'strategic/clear/in control/confident' and 'euphemistic/provisional/trendy', influence how we perceive our managed and mediated 'lifestyle' reality, and more importantly, how we describe and perceive ourselves as part of such a reality?

Strategically managed identity

The division between professional and personal life seems to vanish and is transformed into a 'freely' chosen lifestyle (Rose, 1999), to be managed according to guidelines and 'How To's'. To remain employable, everyone must adapt, and their lifestyle needs to evolve accordingly. To accomplish this, one's (professional) identity must be moulded into a 'sellable self' (Fogde, 2011). This is thought to be best achieved by viewing oneself as if a company, 'ME Inc.' (ibid., p. 70), or a product, a 'brand called "you"' (Hancock & Tyler, 2004, p. 633), which seems closely related to the notion of identity as defined by a leading business school:

> It is the leader – the strategist as meaning maker – who must make vital choices that determine a company's very identity, who says. 'This is our purpose, not that. This is who we will be ... Others, inside and outside a company will contribute in meaningful ways, but in the end it is the leader who bears responsibility for the choices that are made and indeed for the fact that choices are made at all.'
>
> (Montgomery (for McKinsey on Finance), 2012)

This may be translated into: you (jobseeker/career-pursuer/consultant) are advised to view yourself *as* if you are an organisation whose identity[12] you, as a leader, need to strategically manage towards a perceived ideal for the (future) employer/desired customer and to which others, both inside and outside 'ME Inc.', may contribute in meaningful ways, a process in which vital strategic choices need to be made for which, in the end, you alone – the leader – are responsible.

Furthermore, identity appears to be equated with purpose: who we are (choose to be) defines our purpose. Thus, purpose in (perhaps even the ultimate meaning of) life becomes intertwined with careers, rendering employability of immense import. Moreover, when the strategic pursuit is not successful, you alone are to blame. You become a 'have not' in a world where 'haves' are regarded as being successful in professional, social and personal life. The pressure to perform may increase to the point that it can become overwhelming; failure will often lead to self-blame in such a context (Sharone, 2013). Influences from the social environment impacting upon the chances of success (e.g. access to networks, unemployment rates, economical/political situations) tend to be overlooked or deliberately omitted.

Towards a 'sellable self'

Every position/consulting assignment demands the construction of an adjusted, 'discursively constructed' (Fogde, 2011), 'sellable self' in wording that is simultaneously 'strategic/clear/in control/confident', 'euphemistic/provisional' *and* on trend. Besides the difficulty of dealing with these complex, uncertain and sometimes contradictory demands, I challenge the notion that a person's 'sellable' identity can be 'easily constructed'. It seems to me that even the *as if* treatment is problematic: we cannot define our 'purpose' or 'who we are (want to be)' just to suit ourselves; we rely on our *socio-political* environment to make sense of our identity:

> Because of the very nature of the human condition – that we can only define ourselves in exchange with others, those who bring us up, and those whose society we come to see as constitutive of our identity – our self-understanding always places us among others. The placements differ greatly, and understanding these differences and their change is the stuff of history.
>
> (Taylor, 1992, p. 257)

Our understanding of who we are is derived from being with (groups of) people. Our understanding of self emerges in ongoing processes of gesture and response (Mead, 1992) with others. Our interaction with people informs us about ourselves (as adapted to specific circumstances). Gaining such an understanding of who we are (expect to be) in certain situations/groups in a particular organisation would inevitably be, even with the help of a coach, extremely complicated.

I appreciate the need to present ourselves differently in different places. For different 'audiences', as Goffman illustrates in *The Presentation of Self in Everyday Life* (Goffman, 1959/1990), it is natural that we co-operate and compete (Elias, 2001, p. 48) to achieve goals. However, our 'sellable selves' go beyond this. These co-created images are not just a slightly polished presentation. We turn the social adaptation of self (Elias, 2000) 'artificially' into over-idealised selves, similar to the glossy images in an advertising brochure. This glossy image may perhaps be as attractive to ourselves as we believe it to be for potential employers/principals; feeling insecure and anxious about finding a job/assignment in such a competitive market, the manipulation of my image certainly boosted my self-confidence to some degree. This effect, however, soon subsided whenever I imagined my 'match' with this image being assessed eye to eye in a job interview, what Goffman describes as the 'crucial concern' of 'whether it will be credited or discredited' (Goffman, 1959/1990, p. 245).

My enhanced image did not fit comfortably with the way I saw myself or talked, even when in important negotiations. I felt like plastic surgery taken too far: what had begun as minor modifications to my image, carried out iteratively over successive applications, resulted in a gradual sense of alienation, difficult to specify:

> Perhaps instead of talking about identities, inherited or acquired, it would be more in keeping with the realities of the globalizing world to speak of identification, a never-ending, always incomplete, unfinished and open-ended activity in which we all, by necessity or by choice, are engaged.
> (Bauman, 2002, p. 11)

Perhaps it is through compensating for uncertainty and unpredictability with confident, but still provisional and euphemistic, text and talk, we are kept, and at the same time keep ourselves, in motion, continuously and painstakingly developing ourselves to stay aligned with anticipated but uncertain future demands in pursuit of an 'optimal lifestyle'.

Conclusion

My aim in this chapter has not been to deny the need/desire to pursue goals nor the wish to further one's career. Career coaching and consultancy processes are certainly a means of supporting people (in organisations) in achieving goals. Rather, I have drawn attention to the way in which the pursuit of goals (with the help of experts) is commonly portrayed, the managerialist approach: strategically plan and control to achieve clear goals, following *a* right way, having crystal clear aims and making rational decisions to get to preferred outcomes.

Making ourselves attractive to organisations by making use of glossy images as a jobseeker bears some similarity to how we market ourselves and our tools and techniques as consultants by means of fashionable propositions: in doing this, we self-govern our performance. Holding on to our strategically created glossy image and brilliantly simple x-step procedures, and making use of the fashionable conversational patterns that support these, may lead to alienation of our self and self-doubt. Can we live up to this image? This focus on our image and tooling may distract us from what is really going on between us and what we regard as meaningful. Covering over the 'messiness' of everyday life/practice, neglecting our interdependency and interrelatedness that enables and restricts us and the intricacies of the games that we become immersed in may lead to anxiety and self-blame. We need to be able to make sense of what we are trying to achieve together. Of major importance in this is understanding words as action and that words mediate our reality, pointing to the (huge) impact certain conversational patterns may have in a consulting practice. We need to bear in mind the potential consequences of this.

Forming such understanding, we may feel overwhelmed by the complexity of social networks that we may be anxious to join or work in. In actual practice, these are no more than the small groups of people we find ourselves in direct relation with. Whilst such groups, in turn, do form part of a large and complex society, we should keep in mind that this is a society in which no single individual or group can ever predict or control the future or its shifting demands. This is what I try to pay attention to in my practice, around research and innovation, at times a multi-stakeholder environment in which it is impossible to get a full understanding of the intricacies of 'the game of games' (Mowles, 2015, p. 108) let alone manage these. It helps me when I pay attention to what *is*, stay alert to what emerges in processes and procedures, to ways in which my expert role may influence our (possibilities for) interaction, to the perspectives of people I work with and how we use text and talk – all of this to enable the co-creation of meaningful descriptions of the socio-political context of our work (environment) and ourselves (as part of it) and what this all means in relation to the goals we set.

Notes

1. This chapter presents work that was first explored in the author's 2016 doctoral thesis entitled "Becoming Savvy: Developing Awareness of Everyday Politics" available at https://doi.org/10.18745/th.17116.
2. The dual career network was set up by a number of large multinational organisations in order to help integration of spouses of expat employees into Swiss society and (if applicable) find a job.
3. Service providers in this case were independent advisors, career coaches.
4. In this specific case, counselling is offered too; however, describing this in more detail is beyond the scope of this chapter.
5. At the Swedish white-collar union, Sif.
6. I will return to this in the section on Identity.
7. Explained further on.
8. 'Societies in which the division of functions is more or less advanced, in which the chains of action binding individuals together are longer and the functional dependencies between people greater' (Elias, 2000, p. 370).
9. Someone is maze-bright when he or she is capable of (quickly) forming an understanding of the organisational 'map' of all stakeholders, people forming the organisation, of their needs and expectations, their duties, stances, responsibilities, the products made and services offered, organisational issues and so on, more or less knowing their way around.
10. 'there may be multiple games being played at the same time' (Mowles, 2015).
11. Our intentions, expectations, hopes (etc.) influence our perception.
12. This seems to work interchangeably: the organisational identity can be viewed *as if* a person.

References

Abrahamson, E. (1996) Management Fashion. *Academy of Management Review*, 21(1), pp. 254–285.

Alvesson, M. & Karreman, D. (2000) Varieties of Discourse: On the Study of Organizations Through Discourse Analysis. *Human Relations*, 53(8), pp. 1125–1149.

Bauman, Z. (2002) Identity in the Globalizing Word. In: E. Ben-Rafael & Y. Sternberg, eds. *Identity, Culture and Globalization*. Leiden: Die Deutsche Bilbiothek – CIP-Einheitsaufnahme, pp. 471–482.

Birnbaum, R. (2000) The Life Cycle of Academic Management Fads. *The Journal of Higher Education*, 71(1), pp. 1–16.

Bourdieu, P. (2003) *Practical Reason: On the Theory of Action*. Cambridge: Polity Press.

Bourdieu, P. & Wacquant, L. J., 1992. *An Invitation to Reflexive Sociology*. 2007 ed. Cambridge: Polity Press.

Cheek (for LearnVest-Forbes), D. (2013) *10 Things You Should Know About Career Coaching*. [Online]. Available at: http://www.forbes.com/sites/learnvest/2013/07/09/10-things-you-should-know-about-career-coaching/ [Accessed 27 August 2014].

Clark, A., Georgellis, Y. & Sanfey, P. (2001) Scarring: The Psychological Impact of Past Unemployment. *Economica*, 68(270), pp. 221–241.

Council of the European Union (2008) *Council Resolution on Better Integrating Lifelong Guidance into Lifelong Learning Strategies*. Brussels: Council of the European Union.

Cremin, C. (2009) Never Employable Enough: The (Im)possibility of Satisfying the Boss's Desire. *Organization*, 17(2), pp. 131–149.

Darmon, I. & Perez, C. (2010) 'Conduct of conduct' or the Shaping of 'Adequate Dispositions'? Labour Market and Career Guidance in Four European Countries. *Critical Social Policy*, 31(1), pp. 77–101.

Elias, N. (1956) Problems of Involvement and Detachment. *The British Journal of Sociology*, 7(3), pp. 226–252.

Elias, N. (1978) *What Is Sociology?* New York: Columbia University Press.

Elias, N. (2000) Part Four: Synopsis: Towards a Theory of Civilizing Processes State Formation and Civilization. In: *The Civilizing Process*. E. Dunning, J. Goudsblom & S. Mennell, eds. Malden (MA): Blackwell Publishing.

Elias, N. (2001) Part I: The Society of Individuals. In: *The Society of Individuals*. M. Schröter, ed. New York/London: Continuum.

Fleck, L. (1979) *Genesis and Development of a Scientific Fact*, Chicago, IL: University of Chicago Press,

Fogde, M. (2011) Governing Through Career Coaching: Negotiations of Self-Marketing. *Organization*, 18(1), pp. 65–82.

Gandolfi, F. (2009) Executing Downsizing: The Experience of Executioners. *Contemporary Management Research*, 5(2), pp. 185–200.

Goffman, E. (1959/1990) *The Presentation of Self in Everyday Life*. London: Penguin Books.

Hancock, P. & Tyler, M. (2004) 'MOT Your Life': Critical Management Studies and the Management of Everyday Life. *Human Relations*, 57(5), pp. 619–645.

Hareli, S. & Tzafrir, S. (2006) The Role of Causal Attributions in Survivors' Emotional Reactions to Downsizing'. *Human Resource Development Review*, 5(4), pp. 1–22.

Herr, E. L., Cramer, S. H. & Niles, S. G. (2003) *Career Guidance and Counseling Through the Lifespan: Systematic Approaches*. 6th ed. Boston (MA): Pearson Education Inc.

Intermediair (2014) *http://www.intermediair.nl* [Online], Available: http://www.intermediair.nl [Accessed 8 December 2014].

Jackall, R. (2010) *Moral Mazes, the World of Corporate Managers*. 20th anniversary ed. New York: Oxford University Press, Inc.

Krejsler, J. (2007) Discursive Strategies That Individualize: CVs and Appraisal Interviews. *International Journal of Qualitative Studies in Education*, 20(4), pp. 473–490.

Mead, G. H. (1992) *Mind, Self, & Society: From the Standpoint of a Social Behaviourist*. Chicago: the University of Chicago Press, Ltd., London.

Montgomery (for McKinsey on Finance), C. (2012) How Strategists Lead. *McKinsey on Finance*, Summer. Issue 44.

Mowles, C. (2015) *Managing in Uncertainty – Complexity and the Paradoxes of Everyday Organizational Life*. 1st ed. Oxon: Routledge.

Orwell, G. (1987) 'The Principles of Newspeak' an Appendix to 1984. In: *Complete Works of George Orwell*. 1987 ed. London: Penguin Books Ltd.

Rose, N. (1999) *Governing the Soul: The Shaping of the Private Self*. 2nd ed. London: Free Association Books.

Sharone, O. (2013) Why Do Unemployed Americans Blame Themselves While Israelis Blame the System? *Social Forces*, 91(4), pp. 1429–1450.

Shaw, P. (2002) *Changing Conversations in Organizations: A Complexity Approach to Change*. Oxon: Routledge - Taylor & Francis Group.

Sidiropoulou-Dimakakou, D., Mylonas, K. M., Argyropoulou, K. & Drosos, N. (2013) Career Decision-Making Characteristics of Primary Education Students in Greece. *International Education Studies*, 6(5), pp. 22–32.

Spicer, A. S. (2013) Shooting the Shit: The Role of Bullshit in Organisations. *M@n@gement*, 16(5), pp. 653–666.

Stacey, R. D., Griffin, D. & Shaw, P. (2000) *Complexity and Management: Fad or Radical Challenge to Systems Thinking?* London: Routledge.

Taylor, C. (1992) *Modernity and the Rise of the Public Sphere*. Stanford: Stanford University.

The National Black MBA Association (2014) *National Black MBA Association Inc. – Empowering Visionaries*. [Online] Available at: http://www.nbmbaa.org/programs/ntential/Default.aspx [Accessed 8 December 2014].

Wilkinson, M. (2019) *The Secrets of Facilitation*. Available at https://www.leadstrat.com/facilitators/michael-wilkinson/ [Accessed 18 December 2021]

CONCLUSION

SUMMARISING REFLECTIONS ON THE PRACTICE OF CONSULTANCY

Karina Solsø and Nicholas Sarra

Each of the chapters within this book has focused on its unique theme, drawing from the experience and curiosity of the author. Yet, at the same time there are particular themes which permeate this volume. All the chapters have offered a questioning and a critique of a consultancy style, which aims for alignment, positivity, harmony and an idealised future. The experience of being on the receiving end of this consultancy style is poignantly captured in Janssen's contribution.

Most often, theories that come to gain prominence in the management discourse involve a good amount of simplification, for example, emphasizing aligned forms of leadership, widely shared values that are agreed upon by everyone, clear descriptions of roles and responsibility, tools and models. Such simplifications make us prone to unforeseen frustrations and surprises or – perhaps – if we take the emotional quality of experience into consideration, disappointment or disillusionment. This is typically when what actually happens diverges from the plan to a degree that can make both consultants and their clients lose a sense of confidence and feeling of

DOI: 10.4324/9781003095941-8

competence. In much literature on consultancy, the messiness of everyday interactions, the political power struggles, the gameplaying, the agonistic and conflictual qualities of interaction often get covered over or neglected. When the unexpected does arise and the best-laid plans and strategies go awry, then all involved may experience a sense of failure or humiliation.

What these chapters have in common is a reflexive inquiry into the experience of some sort of breakdown (Agar, 1986; Brinkmann, 2012). Breakdowns emerge when our habitual ways of thinking and acting turn out to be insufficient to render us able to respond to the situations that we face (Dewey, 1922). Whenever such a breakdown happens, our routinized ways of responding in the living present are disrupted, which is often a painful experience. This quality of psychological painfulness can be understood as an emotional response to a disruption to the sense of self, of who we understand ourselves to be in relation to the lifeworld and our positioning within it. Thus, the dynamics of identity may be writ large in consultancy encounters as represented through the preceding chapters. When identities are experienced as at stake, then people may respond as if an existential threat is underway and fight accordingly for the maintenance of a self-affirming status quo.

However, this disrupted sense of order and routine can also allow for the emergence of an opportunity for reflection; for more nuanced and rigorous ways of making sense of experience; for calling into question assumptions and pre-understandings. Hence, the chapters here speak to the significance of the consultant's forbearance of uncertainty and negative capability, that is, 'being in uncertainties, mysteries, doubts, without any irritable reaching after fact and reason' (John Keats 1817 letter to his brothers George and Tom).

The chapters have demonstrated a robust reflective inquiry into the lived experience of the messy and complex reality of consultants, a reality which inevitably involves an engagement with the everyday politics that arise as a consequence of the human condition of plurality (Arendt, 1958). An inquiry into these breakdowns reveals particular assumptions, which are then called into question.

The role of conflict and agonistic relationships

Consultancy is often perceived to be successful if it is characterized by an absence of conflict and critique. The relationship between client and consultant is supposed to be a collaborative and positive one, as Masselink draws attention to in Chapter 5. A particular responsibility which consultants take on is to create a sense of collaboration in the relationship with their clients. This sense of collaboration is influenced by the expectations of monetary transaction. People generally pay for consultancy and they expect a product, which can deliver added value. This commodified aspect of consultancy is difficult to ignore, as it is an essential quality in the interdependent relationship (Elias, 1939/2000) between client and consultant. However, rejecting or denying the competitive, conflictual, agonistic element of the relationship means denying its political-ethical character. Human interaction is paradoxically cooperative and conflictual (Mead, 1934); being willing to engage in conflict can mean that one cares enough not to compromise in situations where one feels that compromise isn't the right solution.

Rather than covering over such conflictual aspects of interaction, this book has suggested that it may be worthwhile paying attention to the generative tensions that arise through the engagement with a plurality of views. Collaborative inquiry into the experience of engaging with difference may generate novel understanding: What is going on? What is at stake? What competing values are being negotiated? What patterns of belonging are being tested?

This attention to the plurality of views and their negotiation through consultancy may be our best chance to develop a degree of objectivity on the world. We occupy unique temporal and spatial experiences as individuals, and as such perceive 'the truth' of organizational process through a plurality of perspectives, which create a style of objectivity. We use 'style' here in Fleck's sense (1979) that individual thoughts represent wider enculturated thought collectives and styles which possess their own historical contingencies. However, the organisational quest for unanimity, alignment and consensus can reduce the pluralism required for objectivity to a singularity (Arendt, 1958), which in extremis may constitute a form of tyranny through which any pluralistic consultancy gestures may be silenced through the ideal of neutrality. This silencing or masking of the consultant's attitudinal dispositions creates dilemmas for their capacity to act as moral agents and to respond to the emergent ethics of the consultancy encounter, as both Chauhan and Solsø draw attention to in their chapters.

The ideal of neutrality covers over ethical concerns

When consultants get involved in an organization, there is a generalized expectation that they will be neutral. This ideal of neutrality is conceived as a guarantee for a moral practice, in which there is an expectation that the consultant not take sides with a particular subgroup, but will always keep the interest of the company in view. However, this is yet another example of the simplification that pervades the literature on consultancy. In practice, one rarely experiences a single organisational or company interest. Both Masselink and Chauhan describe how the expectation that the consultant acts neutrally has the potential to negate the moral significance of the consultant in situations in which they need to take a position. The consultant may find themselves more pragmatically in situations where the ethics of what to do and what to say emerge through the process (Griffin, 2002). They may have to perform an apparent neutrality in order to appear plausible, but should remain reflexive and responsive to the inevitability of their own prejudice, which may be deeply informative about what may be at stake and which furthermore may guide their inclinations to act. As Curtis has pointed out, the psychological pressures on the consultant can be intense and self-silencing with a tendency to fall back upon various rules and rationalisations which provide an illusion of safety and control. There may be however just a reiteration or reenactment of existing patterns of relating which produce a feeling of stuckness or hopelessness and render the consultant through their supposed neutrality, morally impotent. The consultant may need therefore to move beyond the idea of neutrality in order to improvise and respond more freely to the politics of the situation. This capacity to respond and improvise allows the capacity to acquire like other participants the moral agency to take positions and exert influence.

Mead (1934) makes a normative statement that if an act or judgement is to be considered fully moral, then it should take as many goods and point of view into account as possible. Furthermore, he encourages a practice where one acknowledges one's own partiality, which means being aware of the temptation to ignore certain interests and emphasize others (p. 387). This awareness of one's partiality, however, does not mean that one remains neutral and detached from the political game that is being played. Consultants can't avoid getting caught up in relational power struggles. As soon as the consultant enters an organization, (s)he is already involved in chains of interdependent relationships (Elias, 1991). Consultancy activities take place through the interweaving of intentions from which patterns arise. Rather than avoiding or ignoring this immersion in the pattern, these chapters have encouraged a practice of 'taking experience seriously' through which one engages reflexively with the critical questions that emerge from one's inevitable involvement with the emergent politics, questions that have to do with the competing goods being negotiated.

Acknowledging that ethical practice involves the bringing together of competing goods involved in moral judgments creates a different situation for the consultant. The question of ethics can't be reduced to 'doing what is best for the company', because the whole idea of the company as reduced to economic value through increased productivity is in itself an abstraction, which covers over the variety of values involved in the social phenomena that we call 'a company'. Rather, ethics become a question of taking a variety of needs and values (including one's own) into view.

The role of politics

Just like consultants are expected to have positive and collaborative relationships with their clients, they are also not supposed to get involved with the politics of the organization. Rather, they are supposed to rise above the politics (Mowles, 2011). However, if politics have to do with the power relationships that people form as they engage in relationships with each other, one has to realize that change doesn't happen in the absence of relationships of power, that is, political, but through them. The question for the consultant shifts from being about rising above the power game to a question about how to engage with and make sense of such central phenomena.

Since consultancies most often involve some form of expectation about change, what materializes in practice is the threat of disruption to established patterns of interaction, which will often be experienced as ruptures and displacements of the power relationships and hierarchies. Status, identity and patterns of belonging may be in a process of renegotiation, which can lead to increased anxiety and resistance as the social order suddenly may come to feel fragile. In such situations, feelings of insecurity and uncertainty may abound, which at the same time may also be permeated with excitement and hope for a new order. Since consultants play a key role in the facilitation of such change processes, they can easily find their clients' anxieties and insecurities located with themselves. The risk of exclusion and the potential shame arising from being excluded is an ongoing quality of the work of consultants who are liable to scapegoating dynamics. The team may find a sense of cohesiveness and an amelioration of conflict through the discovery of the consultant as a common enemy or denigrate the processes which they are perceived to have devised.

When this occurs, it is often tempting to try to establish a sense of belonging that overcomes the conflict or the discomfort that the risk of exclusion brings about. It is in such situations, where consultants are powerfully embedded in the politics of belonging that being able to take a 'detour via detachment', as Elias (1987) has it, can be a powerful resource.

Inquiry into affectual qualities of experience

Taking a 'detour via detachment' is Elias's description of reflective processes. According to him, our participation in interaction with others is paradoxically involved and detached, involved in the sense that we are invested in interactions in ways that can produce intense embodied or affectual reactions. However, at the same time, we have the capacity to detach from our involvement, which creates the ability to become reflective about what we have become involved in.

Socialized into thinking that one is supposed to be an independent and autonomous individual, rising above the potential power struggles and tensions, one might easily experience feelings of shame, embarrassment and anxiety when an emergent reality starts to differ from the anticipations of achieved plans and goals. In such moments, one realizes the risk of being constructed as not competent enough. This can evoke anxieties about exclusion, potential ridicule and denigration. Anticipating such uncomfortable affectual experiences can easily be so threatening that the consultant withdraws from the heat of a situation, since such experiences will feel like signposts of failure. A projective process may ensue in which the consultant comes to embody the collective vulnerabilities of the group and may come to identify and believe their sense of vulnerability to be purely personal as opposed to having arisen through the relational context.

This book has offered a radically alternative interpretation of such affectual experiences. Becoming aware of the notion that powerful affectual experiences are not unusual materializations of the political engagement with difference can be helpful in terms of making sense of them in the spur of the moment. Masselink suggests that we think about these dilemmas as 'a politics of affect', which creates an opportunity for consultants to work collaboratively with their clients and to reflect upon the ways in which affectual responses can evoke important insights about what might be going on and what may be at stake for those involved.

Implications for consultancy method

What then are the implications for consultancy method in the above conclusions?

There are strong themes in these chapters of the significance of plurality and the consequential politics of engaging with difference for the consultant. It is suggested that these processes may contribute to a variety of psychosomatic pressures upon consultants, which require a capacity for reflexivity in order to keep a sense of ground in a potentially turbulent landscape. Reflexivity may be thought about as the fluctuating capability to think about the way we are thinking/feeling.

Reflexivity here is taken to be a social process both intra- and interpersonally with the mind itself following Mead (1934). As such, a reflexive practice encompasses the imagined emotional and attitudinal tendencies of the other.

Pragmatically, consultancy as a reflexive practice thus highlights the importance of consultants themselves being able to access places to think things through with others who are not themselves immersed in the direct power relations of their particular consultancies, whether this be in professional communities of practice, supervisory fora or training as well as educational programmes. We have seen in the above chapters the various pressures on consultants to behave in ways which the group deems acceptable as a means of belonging, that is, being able to say and think about certain things or express particular attitudes and not being able to say or even to think about some matters. This is so particularly for interventions, which might impact upon the status quo functions of the group.

The reflexive process, or as Elias puts it, the detour via detachment (Elias, 1987), provides the potential means through which the various maelstroms of organizational consultancy can be endured and engaged with creatively.

The task may then be thought about not so much as having to sort things out, find solutions, keep the customer happy and so on, although these qualities will often play a role and be achieved. However, being able to think, feel and understand more deeply the consultancy situations in which one is involved becomes a highly important practice. These qualities of thinking, feeling and deepening understanding of one's own involvement require a developing understanding of others' thoughts, feelings and understandings through which greater capacity for freedom of action may arise.

So often, everything in consultancy work is focused upon the plan, the agreed action, some imagined outcome of the process. The consultant themselves inevitably experiences the social patterning of the group they work with in an embodied way. They resonate with emotional themes which interact with her or his own history. Thus, they find themselves inducted into specific power relations. This sense of induction tends to suggest what it is that is required to belong to or be excluded with that specific group situation. The interaction of the participants themselves, including the consultant, as the means through which the future is constructed, can be lost in plain sight. We suggest that reflections on the ways in which consultants experience this social patterning deserve more attention than what is often the case.

We hope that the readers, many of whom will be working consultants, have found this volume helpful as a means to the recognition and validation of issues often neglected in the consultancy literature. Perhaps, they may find the experiences related here, enable them to sustain further the intense emotional work frequently evoked through consultancy practice and to find further understanding in situations where there may be concerted efforts to restrict and limit the possibilities of meaning and human agency.

References

Agar, M. (1986). *Speaking Ethnography*. Thousand Oaks, CA: SAGE

Arendt, H. (1958). *The Human Condition*. Chicago, IL: University of Chicago Press.

Brinkmann, S. (2012). *Qualitative Inquiry in Everyday Life: Working with Everyday Life Materials*. London: SAGE.

Dewey, J. (1922) *Human Nature and Conduct: An Introduction to Social Psychology.* New York: Warren Press.

Elias, N. (1987) *Involvement and Detachment.* Oxford: Blackwell. MIT Press.

Elias, N. (1991) *The Society of Individuals.* Oxford: Blackwell Publishing.

Elias, N. (1939/2000) *The Civilizing Process.* Oxford: Blackwell Publishing.

Fleck, L. (1979) *Genesis and Development of a Scientific Fact.* Chicago, IL: University of Chicago Press.

Griffin, D. (2002). *The Emergence of Leadership: Linking Self-Organization and Ethics.* London: Routledge.

Mead, G. H. (1934). *Mind, Self and Society from the Standpoint of a Social Behaviorist.* Chicago, IL: University of Chicago Press.

Mowles, C. (2011). *Rethinking Management: Radical Insights from the Complexity Sciences.* Farnham: Gower Applied Research.

INDEX

Note: Information in figures and tables is indicated by page numbers in *italics* or **bold**.

action: in Arendt 90; degradation of, in favor of work 91–92
action research 2
advice 138–139
agency: assertion of 17; compliance and 100; emotion and 6; human experience and 28; neutrality and 11–12, 156; other and 80; of self-constraint 53; shame and 31
agenda, for away-day 42–43
agonistic relationships 154–155
alignment 54, 77, 98, 155
Appreciative Inquiry 8–9
Arendt, Hannah 84–85, 88–92, 96–99, 102–103
away-day 41–50

balloon exercise 47–50
Bernstein, Richard 101
Briigs, Katharine Cook 47
Brown, Brene 42

career coaching 134–136
CAS *see* complex adaptive systems (CAS)
chairing conference 110–111
Civilising Process, The (Elias) 30
client relationship: active-passive 107–108; functionalising 108–110
cognitivist psychology 46
collaboration: as affective ethics 118–120; in context of consulting 107–108; freedom and 121–122; interdependency and 111–113; normalisation of 105–106; as politics of affect 105–123
competing goods 26–30, 157
complexity: butterfly effect and 28; collaboration and 108; of mandates 91; realisation of, hopelessness and 87; of social interaction 5, 10, 22; of social networks 148

INDEX

complex responsive processes 65–67, 75, 128
compliance 21, 50, 56, 98, 106, 118
conflict 10–11, 29, 53, 60, 66, 74–75, 77, 79–80, 98, 154–155
conversational patterns 140
co-operation 105–106
countertransference 23–24

Descartes, René 71
detachment 19, 132–133, 158–159
Dewey, John 51, 71, 112, 114, 154
dialogic approaches 19, 22
disagreement 10, 68, 95
dissent 10
diversity 22, 77–79, 116, 130
dualism 69, 71, 79–80

Eichmann, Adolph 89
Elias, Norbert 30, 53, 66, 76, 132, 158
engaged fallibilistic plurality 101, 103
ethics: collaboration as affective 118–120; of competing goods 26–30; deontological 26; judging and 28–29; normative 26; pragmatic 29–30; utilitarian 26
exclusion 6, 9–10, 12, 17, 32–33, **34**, 77, 79, 113, 158
experience: affectual qualities of 158–159; perceptual gaps and 20–21

facilitation: of away-day 41–50; of change processes 158; defined 39–40; routine of 123; as social object 40; as temporary leadership 56–57
fallibilism 6, 28, 101, 103
fragmentation 88, 95, 108
freedom: collaboration and 121–122; powerlessness and 84–88, 93, 97–98, 102; publicness and 99; we-ness and 102

game, metaphor of 133–134
Goffman, Erving 7, 146–147
goods, competing 26–30
governing 136–138
Griffin, Douglas 51, 60, 62, 65–66, 69, 75–76, 92, 156

harmony 9, 77, 98–99, 113, 153
Hegel, Georg 67, 78
Honneth, Axel 60, 62, 65, 67
hopelessness 12, 87–88, 93, 156

identity: in Arendt 92; co-operation and 68; experience and 21; in groups 52; I/Me dialectic and 51–52, 66; pragmatism and 20; purpose and 145–146; self-consciousness and 51; strategically managed 145–147
ideology 10, 32–33, **34**, 66, 81, 105, 107, 109, 112–113, 129
I/Me dialectic 52–53
Immunity to Change 74
improvisation 4, 8, 156
inclusion 77–79, 83
infantilisation 50, 55–56
inquiry, reflective 1, 11, 101–102, 154
instrumentalism 3–8
instrumental rationality 3, 12, 46, 90, 92–93, 99–100
interdependency 79–80, 83, 141, 155

joblessness 128–129
judging, ethics and 28–29
Jung, Carl 47

Kant, Immanuel 97
Keats, John 154

labour: in Arendt 90; cognitive *vs.* emotional 73

INDEX

leadership development programme 62–65, 76

management theory 30, 83–84
managerialism 26, 141
MBTI see Myers Briggs type indicator (MBTI)
Mead, George Herbert 9–10, 17, 20–21, 28–29, 31, 39–40, 52, 54, 71, 156
Mowles, Chris 3, 5, 9, 11, 51, 53, 55–57, 83, 92, 100–101, 141, 148–149, 157
Myers, Isabel Briggs 47
Myers Briggs type indicator (MBTI) 40–42, 46–47

neutrality 20–21, 156–157

OD see Organisation Development (OD)
Open Space Technology (OST) 27, 34
open systems tradition 23
Organisation Development (OD) 2–3; collaboration in 107; dialogic approaches to 19, 22; instrumentalism in 3–8; tools in 3–8
OST see Open Space Technology (OST)
otherness 77–79, 101, 103, 114, 119–120
Owen, Harrison 27

paradox/paradoxical 7, 13, 28, 31, 52–53, 60, 66–72, 75, 77, 79–80, 106, 108, 133, 140–141, 158
perceptual gaps 20–21
plurality: actualising 12, 85, 98–99; as dynamic 97; engaged fallibilistic 101, 103; of interaction 11; public realm and 96–98

political action, consultancy as 99–101
politics: role of 157–158
positivism 5
positivity 2, 8, 62, 67, 84, 153
postmodernism 20, 23
power: abuse of 97; asymmetries 65; differential 108, 117, 133; disciplinary 46; in groups 55–56; negotiations of 9; patterning of 10; positions 101; recognition and 68, 79; relationships and 7, 66, 75–76, 106, 112–113, 133, 157; struggles 154, 156, 158
powerlessness 84–88, 93, 97–98, 102
practical judgement 73, 120
pragmatism 11, 17, 20–21, 29–30, 32, 35, 71, 118
Presentation of Self in Everyday Life, The (Goffman) 146–147
Probyn, Elspeth 31–32
process consultation 18–19
Psychological Types (Jung) 47
publicness 99

recognition: derived from work 129; misrecognition and 71–72; as non-teleological concept 65–66; processes of 75–78; theories of 67–68
reflection 101–102, 115–118, 159–160
reflective inquiry 1, 11, 101–102, 154
reflexivity 10, 16–17, 23, 121, 159
relating 66–67
responsibility 89–90, 97, 144
Rogers, Carl 39

Schein, Edgar 18, 62
self: governing 136–138; joblessness and 128–129; sellable 146–147; strategically-managed identity and 145–147

shame 17; in away-day 41–42; conceptualization of 30–32; defining 51–52; infantilisation and 50; learning and 52–53; as opportunity to inquire 30–35, **34**; reflexive inquiries into experiences of 32–33; solitary 51; working together to avoid risk of 53–57
Shaw, Patricia 6, 60, 65–66, 75, 84, 101, 140
simplification 69
social networks 148
social object: consulting as 21–26; facilitation as 40
spontaneity 28, 31, 51, 73
Stacey, Ralph 3–5, 11, 28, 46, 51, 54, 60, 62, 65–66, 69, 75–76, 78, 83, 90–92, 100, 128
strategic choice theory 46
strategic management 129, 135, 138, 140–145
stuckness 93–95

Taylor, Charles 88
T-group 2
Thomason, Krista 31
360 feedback reports 45
Tomkins, Silvan 32
tools, practical 71–74

uncertainty 1, 3–8, 61, 70, 100–101, 103, 107–108, 119, 142, 147, 157
unemployment 128–129
utilitarian ethics 26

values 8–10, 28–29, 62, 122–123, 137, 143, 157
vulnerability 43–44

we-ness 102
work: in Arendt 90; degradation of action in favour of 91–92; recognition derived from 129
World War II 89

Lightning Source UK Ltd.
Milton Keynes UK
UKHW012208221122
412683UK00008B/49